DEFENSE OF MARRIAGE:
DOES IT NEED DEFENDING?

D1713912

DEFENSE OF MARRIAGE: DOES IT NEED DEFENDING?

JAMES PERKINS
EDITOR

Novinka Books
New York

Production Coordinator: Tatiana Shohov
Coordinating Editor: Tatiana Shohov
Senior Production Editors: Susan Boriotti and Donna Dennis
Production Editors: Marius Andronie and Rusudan Razmadze
Office Manager: Annette Hellinger
Graphics: Levani Chlaidze and Magdalena Nuñez
Editorial Production: Alexandra Columbus, Maya Columbus, Robert Brower,
     Vladimir Klestov and Lorna Loperfido
Circulation: Luis Aviles, Raymond Davis, Cathy DeGregory, Melissa Diaz,
     Ave Maria Gonzalez, Marlene Nuñez, Jeannie Pappas,
     Vera Popovic and Frankie Punger
Communications and Acquisitions: Serge P. Shohov

✱

Library of Congress Cataloging-in-Publication Data
Available Upon Request

ISBN: 1-59454-074-8.   KF   5 11
         . D44   2004

Copyright © 2004 by Novinka Books, An Imprint of
     Nova Science Publishers, Inc.
     400 Oser Ave, Suite 1600
     Hauppauge, New York 11788-3619
     Tele. 631-231-7269   Fax 631-231-8175
     e-mail: Novascience@earthlink.net
     Web Site: http://www.novapublishers.com

Printed in the United States of America

CONTENTS

PREFACE

The contemporary world has become so unraveled that the Congress of the United States, with nothing better to do, has felt the necessity of passing a Defense of Marriage Act. We are all being treated to daily media coverage of the same-sex marriages and programming which would make the devil blush. We are being told that the weird is just fine. Will the children of the man-women unions see this deviation as normal? Some critics blame society's depravation on the legions of spent politicians wreaking havoc on the country and perhaps they are not wrong. But maybe, just maybe, society in the main has had enough and is at last fighting back against the forces tying to intimidate it. This book looks at laws and actions being taken at the federal level to right a ship gone very wrong.

Chapter one discusses the legal principles applied by courts to determine the validity of a marriage contracted in another state.

Legislation that would prohibit federal recognition of same-sex marriages and allow individual states to refuse to recognize such marriages performed in other states has been considered and approved by the 104th Congress. Called the Defense of Marriage Act, the measure responds to a pending court case in Hawaii that could result in the legalization there of marriages between two persons of the same sex. President Clinton signed the measure into law without ceremony on September 21, 1996 (P.L. 104-199). Chapter two presents this issue.

Chapter three identifies federal laws in which benefits, rights, and privileges are contingent on marital status. Generally all those laws in the United States Code in which marital status is a factor, even though some of these laws may not directly create benefits, rights, or privileges are included.

Currently neither federal nor state law affirmatively allows gay or lesbian couples to marry. Chapter four discusses the Defense of Marriage

Act (DOMA), P.L. 104-199, which prohibits federal recognition of same-sex marriages and allows individual states to refuse to recognize such marriages performed in other states, as well as the potential legal challenges to the DOMA. Moreover the chapter summarizes the legal principles applied in determining the validity of a marriage contracted in another state and surveys the various approaches employed by states to prevent same-sex marriage.

State laws concerning the eligibility of homosexuals to adopt vary. Some states statutorily prohibit such action, while other are silent on the issue, leaving interpretation to the courts. Chapter five summarizes state laws concerning non-relative adoption by homosexual individuals and couples.

Chapter six talks about the Marriage Protection Act, as the bill is known. It removes jurisdiction from certain federal courts over questions pertaining to the 1996 Defense of Marriage Act, better known as DOMA. The legislation was introduced limiting the federal courts' ability to set a national precedent undermining the institution of marriage. DOMA says that no state is required to give full faith and credit to a marriage license issued by another state if that relationship is between two people of the same sex. It also defines the terms "marriage" and "spouse" for purposes of federal law as terms only applying to relationships between people of the opposite sex.

A 4-3 majority of the Supreme Judicial Court of Massachusetts ruled last November in *Goodridge v. Massachusetts Dep't of Health*, 798 N.E. 2d 941 (Mass. 2003), that the state's refusal to issue marriage licenses to same-sex couples violated the state constitution. The court concluded that to insist on traditional marriage was to engage in "invidious" discrimination that the court would not tolerate. The majority, therefore, ruled that marriage must be open to same-sex couples, and delayed the decision for 180 days so that the state legislature could pass laws it "deemed necessary" in light of the decision. Chapter seven discusses this decision and the legalization of same-sex marriages in Massachussetts.

Chapter eight provides background information and analysis of the issues associated with the federal individual income tax and marriage neutrality. Issues addressed include a discussion of the conflicting goals of equity under an income tax, an explanation of the causes of structural marriage penalties and bonuses, an overview of the historical tax treatment of marital status, an analysis of the income splits that produce structural marriage penalties and bonuses, estimates of the magnitude of structural penalties and bonus at various income levels, and an examination of possible legislative solutions.

Chapter nine discusses the 'Defense of Marriage Act' and the different views on the issue.

Chapter ten reviews what many believe is evidence that America is now at a moral crossroads. The news that the Massachusetts Supreme Court has ruled in favor of same-sex marriages in that state is discussed. While the issue is by no means settled, it sets the stage for the battle over redefinition of marriage in America. The institution of marriage is the foundation of the family. And families play a critical role in raising our children, the future of our society.

In chapter eleven the author talks about a way to prevent the federal courts from creating a federal "right" for homosexuals to marry each other. This is the Marriage Protection Act (H.R. 3313), which removes jurisdiction from certain federal courts over questions pertaining to the 1996 Defense of Marriage Act, better known as DOMA.

Chapter 1

INTERSTATE MARRIAGE RECOGNITION AND THE DEFENSE OF MARRIAGE ACT

Gina Marie Stevens

BACKGROUND

This chapter discusses the legal principles applied by courts to determine the validity of a marriage contracted in another State. Issues related to this topic have arisen because of the prospect that same-sex marriage will he legalized in Hawaii,[1] although at present no State permits a same-sex couple to marry, and because of legislation recently introduced - The Defense of Marriage Act ("DOMA"). DOMA defines for federal purposes the words 'marriage' and 'spouse' as applying exclusively to persons of different sex, and permits States to disregard same-sex marriages if they so choose. A brief summary of the legislation follows. A discussion of the Full Faith and Credit Clause of the U.S. Constitution is provided to assist the reader in understanding the constitutional principles that govern interstate recognition of judgments and statutes because many have questioned whether this legislation is a legitimate exercise of Congress' power under the Full Faith and Credit Clause. Second, an overview

---

[1] See, *Baehr v. Lewin,* 852 P.2d 44 (Haw. 1993)(held that sex is a suspect classification and that in the absence of a compelling justification, the state's policy of denying legal recognition to same-sex marriages would violate equal protection of the laws as guaranteed by the Hawaii Constitution). The case has been remanded to the trial court for a trial later this year.

of the law governing the validation of out-of-state marriages is provided. Third, the report summarizes the Supreme Court's recent decision in *Romer v. Evans* on the equal protection rights of gays and lesbians, and provides an analysis of *Romer's* applicability to the Defense of Marriage Act. Finally, the issue of whether the Defense of Marriage Act is an impermissible intrusion by Congress into the domestic relations area which has traditionally been regulated by and reserved to the States under the Tenth Amendment is addressed.

THE DEFENSE OF MARRIAGE ACT

The Defense of Marriage Act was introduced during May in the Senate by Senators Dole and Nickles (S. 1740) and in the House of Representatives (H.R. 3396) by Representative Barr "to define and protect the institution of marriage." Section 2 of the bill, "Powers Reserved to the States", provides that "No State, territory, or possession of the United States, or Indian tribe, shall be required to give effect to any public act, record, or judicial proceeding respecting a relationship between persons of the same sex that is treated as a marriage under the laws of such State ..., or a right or claim arising from such relationship." Section 3 of the bill, "Definition of Marriage", provides that "In determining the meaning of any Act of Congress, or of any ruling, regulation, or interpretation of the various administrative bureaus and agencies of the United States, the word 'marriage' means only a legal union between one man and one woman as husband and wife and the word 'spouse' refers only to a person of the opposite sex who is a husband or wife." On May 15, 1995, the House Judiciary Subcommittee on the Constitution held a hearing on H.R. 3396, the Defense of Marriage Act. On May 30, the Constitution Subcommittee approved the bill.

FULL FAITH AND CREDIT

Article IV, section 1 of the Constitution, the Full Faith and Credit Clause, states:

> Full Faith and Credit shall be given in each State to the public Acts, Records, and judicial Proceedings of every other State; And the Congress

may by general Laws prescribe the Manner in which such Acts, Records and Proceedings shall be proved, and the Effect thereof.[2]

The Clause was adopted by the framers at the Constitutional Convention of 1787 "to coordinate the administration of justice among the several independent legal systems which exist in our Federation."[3] Its purpose was "to alter the status of the several states as independent foreign sovereignties, each free to ignore obligations created under the laws and the judicial proceedings of the others, and to make them integral parts of a single nation."[4] The first sentence of the Clause was derived from the Articles of Confederation.[5] The second sentence was added in response to a suggestion by James Madison that the legislature be given the power to provide for the execution of judgments in other States.[6] His proposition was broadened to include not only judgments, but also acts, records, and judicial proceedings.

The meaning of what constitutes giving "full faith and credit" is the principal issue litigated under the Clause. A useful definition of "full faith and credit" is that it requires each State to give the law of every other State the same faith and credit it gives its own law:

> To give full credit to a law most naturally means to treat it as law—as a judicially enforceable norm of human behavior with judicially enforceable consequences for breach. The additional requirement of "full *faith* and credit" appears to be simply a lawyers' redundancy; "faith and credit" was a phrase used in common law cases on recognition of judgments. But the "faith" requirement also suggests that states must act in .good faith in determining the credit due to sister-state law.

> The most important word in the Clause is "full." A state does not owe some credit, partial credit, or credit where it would be wholly unreasonable to deny credit, which seems to be the Supreme Court's current interpretation. Rather, each state owes *full* faith and credit to the law of sister states. *Full* faith and credit is what a state accords its own law. *Full* faith and credit is the maximum possible credit; it is conceptually impossible to give faith and credit that is more than full. Thus, the Clause is most plausibly read as

---

[2] U.S. Const art. IV, § 1.
[3] Jackson, Robert, *Full Faith and Credit - The Lawyer's Clause of the Constitution,* 45 Columbia L. Rev. 1, 2 (1945).
[4] *Williams v. North Carolina,* 317 U.S. 287, 295 (1942).
[5] See, Nadehnann, Kurt, *Full Faith and Credit To Judgments and Public Acts,* 56 Mich. L. Rev. 22 (1957).

requiring each state to give the law of every other state the same faith and credit it gives its own law, to treat the law of sister states as equal in authority to its own."[7]

The Full Faith and Credit Clause applies principally to judgments, and the interstate recognition and enforcement of judgments. It is settled law that final judgments are entitled to foil faith and credit, regardless of the public policies of other States,[8] provided that the issuing State had jurisdiction over the parties and the subject matter.[9] Judgments subject to future modification, such as child support and child custody orders, are not considered final, and therefore are not entitled to full faith and credit.[10] As discussed below, however, Congress enacted legislation to accord full faith and credit to child custody and child support orders. The Full Faith and Credit Clause has rarely been used by courts to validate marriages because marriages are not "legal judgments." However, as explained further below, courts routinely recognize out-of-state marriages. Full faith and credit can be extended to a declaratory judgment of marriage. An action is usually brought to obtain a declaratory judgment concerning the validity of a marriage when questions incidental to the existence of a marriage (i.e., eligibility for survivor's benefits) must be resolved.

Despite the inclusion of 'public acts' within the Clause, and the feet that the Supreme Court has recognized that a statute is a 'public act' within the meaning of the Full Faith and Credit Clause,[11] the Court has imposed only minimal constraints upon the States in their choice of law decisions. In cases that do not involve interstate enforcement of final judgments, but that involve questions as to which State's statute to apply to the parties or occurrence, the Court has allowed States to apply their own law instead of that of sister States, if the State has significant contact or a significant aggregation of contacts with the parties or occurrence.

[6] See, Cooke, Walter Wheeler, *The Powers of Congress under the Full Faith and Credit Clause,* 28YaleL.J. 421(1919).
[7] Layeoek, Douglass, *Equal Citizens of Equal and Territorial States; The Constitutional Foundations of Choice of Law,* 92 Columbia L, Rev. 249, 296 (1992)(footnotes omitted).
[8] In *Fauntelroy v. Lum,* 210 U.S. 230 (1908) the Supreme Court required Mississippi to give full faith and credit to a Missouri judgment, even though that judgment was based upon a "futures" contract, a transaction which Mississippi had outlawed as against its public policy.
[9] *Restatement (Second) of Conflict of Laws* § 107.
[10] *Restatement (Second) Conflict of Laws* § 109.
[11] Bradford Electric Light Co. v. Clapper, 286 U.S. 145, 154-55 (1932).

In 1935, in *Alaska Packers Ass'n v. Industrial Accident Comm'n*,[12] the Supreme Court recognized that under the Full Faith and Credit Clause a State may apply its own law to a conflict between its law and that of another State when it has a superior interest in doing so. The Court confronted the issue of whether the Full Faith and Credit Clause required California to give effect to Alaska's workmen's compensation statute rather than California's workmen's compensation statute. The Court held that the choice of California law was not "so arbitrary or unreasonable as to amount to denial of due process" because "without a remedy in California Pie] would be remediless," and because of California's interest that the worker not become a public charge. The Court wrote:

> In the case of statutes, the extra-state effect of which Congress has not prescribed, where the policy of one state statute comes into conflict with that of another, the necessity of some accommodation of the conflicting interests of the two states is still more apparent. A rigid and literal enforcement of the full faith and credit clause, without regard to the statute of the forum, would lead to the absurd result that, wherever the conflict arises, the statute of each state must be enforced in the courts of the other, but cannot be in its own. ... In either case, the conflict is the same. In each, rights claimed under one statute prevail only by denying effect to the other. In both the conflict is to be resolved, not by giving automatic effect to the full faith and credit clause, compelling the courts of each state to subordinate its own statutes to those of the other, but by appraising the governmental interests of each jurisdiction, and turning the scale of decision according to their weight.[13]

In another California workmen's compensation case, the Court acknowledged that the "Full Faith and Credit Clause does not here enable one state to legislate for the other or to project its laws across state lines so as to preclude the other from prescribing for itself the legal consequences of acts within it."[14] The Court's decision appeared to be influenced by the California statutory provision which expressly provided that no contract, rule, or regulation shall exempt the employer from compensation fixed by the workmen's compensation act. The two cases appear to say that if California did not have a legitimate interest in the

---

[12] 294 U.S. 532 (1935).

[13] Id. at 547.

[14] *Pacific Employers Ins. Co. v. Industrial Accident Comm'n*, 306 U.S. 493, 501 (1939) (the Court held that the Full Faith and Credit Clause did not preclude California from applying its workmen's compensation statute to a Massachusetts employee injured in a work-related accident in California).

application of its own law, the Full Faith and Credit Clause might compel its court to apply the law of the other state; but so long as California's interest in application of its own law is consistent with due process because it involved a reasonable exercise of state power, that interest may not be defeated by giving full faith and credit to another state's law.

The Court has since abandoned the weighing of interests approach taken in the California cases, and instead examines the relevant contacts of the State with the parties and the occurrence giving rise to the litigation.[15] In 1981, in *Allstate Insurance Co. v. Hague,*[16] the Supreme Court held that a State can apply its own law, rather than the law of the sister-State, so long as it has significant contact or a significant aggregation of contacts, creating State interests, with the parties and the occurrence or transaction such that the application of its law is neither arbitrary nor unfair. In *Allstate,* which lacks a majority opinion, a sharply divided Court affirmed the decision of the Minnesota Supreme Court to apply Minnesota law. The Court upheld Minnesota's application of its own law to invalidate a clause in an insurance policy that was issued in Wisconsin to a Wisconsin resident killed in a Wisconsin automobile accident. The plaintiff in the case sought to recover $45,000 by "stacking" three insurance policies that provided uninsured motorist coverage; Minnesota permitted stacking Wisconsin did not. Justice Brennan's opinion, joined by three Justices, found three significant Minnesota contacts; the decedent's widow had moved to Minnesota after his death, the decedent had worked in Minnesota although the accident was not job related, and the insurer also did business in Minnesota. Justice Stevens concurred in the result, and wrote a opinion separate from the plurality's. He wrote that "the Clause should not invalidate a state court's choice of forum law unless that choice threatens the federal interest in national unity by unjustifiably infringing upon the legitimate interest of another State." He did not believe that any threat to national unity or to Wisconsin's sovereignty ensued from allowing Minnesota to resolve the stacking issue since the insurance policy provided coverage for accidents that might occur in other States. The dissenting opinion, written by Justice Powell (joined by Justices Burger and Rehnquist) stated that the Constitution imposed only a "modest check on state power," that "applies only when there are no significant contacts between the State and the litigation."

---

[15] See, *Nevada v. Hall,* 440 U.S. 410, 424 (1979) (the Court established that "the Full Faith and Credit Clause does not require a State to apply another State's law in violation of its own legitimate public policy.")

[16] 449 U.S. 302 (1981).

Thus, the Supreme Court's current approach to the resolution of choice of law cases involving conflicting state statutes is to examine the significant aggregation of contacts the forum has with the parties and the occurrence or transaction so that the application of the forum's law is neither arbitrary nor unfair. This choice of law approach is used by the courts to resolve interstate statutory disputes.

INTERSTATE RECOGNITION OF MARRIAGE

Questions concerning the validity of an out-of-state marriage are generally resolved without reference to the Full Faith and Credit Clause. As previously discussed, marriages are not regarded as judgments. In the legal sense, marriage is a "civil contract" created by the State that establishes certain duties and confers certain benefits. Validly entering into the contract creates the marital status; the duties and benefits a State attaches to the status are the incidents of that status.

The general rule of validation for different-sex marriages is to look to the law of the place where the marriage was celebrated, *lex celebrationis. A* marriage that satisfies the requirements of the State where it was contracted will usually be held valid everywhere.[17] Many States provide by statute that a marriage that is valid where contracted is valid within the State. At least twenty-three States have adopted language substantially similar to the Uniform Marriage and Divorce Act (UMDA),[18] which states: "All marriages contracted . . . outside this State, that were valid at the time of the contract or subsequently validated by the laws of the place in which they were contracted. . .are valid in this State."[19] Several States provide an exception to this general rule by declaring out-of-state marriages void if against the State's public policy or if entered into with the intent to evade the law of the State. At least eleven states have recently passed legislation prohibiting recognition of out-of-state same-sex marriages.[20]

Section 283 of the Restatement (Second) of Conflicts of Law provides:

---

[17] See, Annotation, 71 A.L.R. 687 (1960).

[18] Arizona, Arkansas, California, Colorado, Connecticut, the District of Columbia, Georgia, Hawaii, Idaho, Illinois, Kansas, Kentucky, Louisiana, Michigan, Minnesota, Montana, Nebraska, New Mexico, North Dakota, South Dakota, Utah, Virginia, Wyoming.

[19] Unif. Marriage and Divorce Act § 210, 9A U.L.A. 147.

[20] Alaska, Arizona, Georgia, Idaho, Illinois, Kansas, Oklahoma, South Carolina, South Dakota, Tennessee, Utah.

(1) The validity of marriage will be determined by the local law of the state which, with respect to the particular issue, has the most significant relationship to the spouses and the marriage under the principles stated in § 6.

(2) A marriage which satisfies the requirements of the state where the marriage was contracted will everywhere be recognized as valid unless it violates the strong public policy of another state which had the most significant relationship to the spouses and the marriage at the time of the marriage.[21]

Section 6 lists several factors to he considered by a court in order to determine which State has the most significant relationship to the spouses and the marriage: the relevant policies of the forum and of other interested states, the protection of justified expectations, predictability, and uniformity of result. The comments to section 283 indicate that a marriage that met the requirements of the State where the marriage was contracted has been held invalid only when it violated a strong public policy of a State where at least one of the spouses was domiciled at the time of such marriage and where both made it their home immediately thereafter.[22]

According to the *Restatement,* the "strong public policy" exception exists where the marriage does not satisfy the requirements of the State with the most significant relationship to the spouses and where as a result the marriage would have been invalid if it had been contracted in that State. The primary issue to be resolved by the State with the most significant relationship to the parties is whether its courts would have invalidated the marriage if the question had come before them. First, the courts must consult the statutes of the State. If the State has a statute which invalidates the out-of-state marriage of its residents, the marriage would be held invalid in the State of the most significant relationship. If the State of the most significant relationship has no such statute, the next question is whether the marriage would be held invalid by the courts of that State by application of their choice of law rules. If no answer can be obtained, it must use its own judgment in determining whether the rule that was not satisfied represents a sufficiently strong policy of the State of the most significant relationship. In the absence of explicit statute or judicial precedent, the only rules that the forum would likely find to embody a sufficiently strong policy of that State to warrant invalidation of an out-of-state marriage are rules such as those which prohibit polygamous marriages, certain incestuous marriages, or the marriages of minors below a

---

[21] *Restatement (Second) Conflicts of ike Law* § 283 (1971).
[22] *Id.* at comment (j).

certain age.[23] However, several states recognize certain types of 'incestuous' marriages (e.g., marriages between first cousins) if the marriage is recognized as valid in the State where it was entered into.[24]

Some States may refuse to recognize same-sex marriages basing their refusal upon the public policy exception. Expressions of public policy may be found in statutes that ban same-sex marriages, in States that prohibit recognition of same-sex marriages entered into in sister States, in States where the Attorneys General have construed their statutory or common law as banning legal recognition of same-sex marriages, and in States that have criminal sodomy laws.[25] On the other hand, the public policy of a State or locality may be interpreted as supporting same-sex unions if the jurisdiction has an anti-discrimination law that protects homosexuals, or if it recognizes domestic partnerships among same-sex couples.[26]

In sum, under generally accepted rules of comity Stales currently possess the authority and the discretion to determine whether to recognize marriages from sister States.

CONGRESS' ENFORCEMENT POWER UNDER THE FULL FAITH AND CREDIT CLAUSE

The drafters of DOMA rely upon the second sentence of the Full Faith and Credit Clause as the source of Congress' authority to legislate concerning the recognition States may give to out-of-state same-sex marriages. The second sentence of the Full Faith and Credit Clause gives Congress the power to prescribe the extrastate effect of public acts, records, and proceedings:[27]

"And the Congress may by general Laws prescribe the Manner in which such Acts, Records and Proceedings shall be proved, and the Effect thereof."

---

[23] See, e.g., *Osoinach v. Watkins*, 180 So. 577 (Ala. 1938)(incestuous marriage invalidated by another state); *People u. Kay*, 252 N.Y.S. 518 (N.Y. 1931)(polygamous marriage invalidated by another state); *Pennegar v. State*, 10 S.W. 305 (Term. 1889)(miscegenous marriage invalidated by another state).

[24] See, Clark, Homer, *The Law of Domestic Relations in the United States* 155-57 (2d ed. 1987).

[25] For further information, see, *Out-of-State Marriage Recognition*, General Distribution Memorandum by Gina Marie Stevens, Library of Congress, Congressional Research Service, February 29, 1996.

[26] See, Hewitt Associates, "Private and Public Employers Offering Domestic Partner Benefits 26-28 (Chicago 1995).

[27] *Mills v. Duryee*, 7 Cranch 481, 485, 11 U.S. 481 (1813); *Pacific Employers Ins. Co. v. Industrial Accident Comm'n*, 306 U.S. 493,502 (1939); *Sun Oil Co. v. Wortman*, 486 U.S. 717,729 (1988); *Thompson v. Thompson*, 484 U.S. 174, 182-83 (1988).

As stated earlier, the legislative history of the second sentence of the Clause indicates that the second sentence was added in response to a suggestion by James Madison that the legislature be authorized to provide for the execution of judgments in other States. A resolution was then introduced incorporating Madison's suggestion that provided that the legislature shall by general laws determine the proof and effect of such acts, records, and proceedings.[28] The intent of the Framers was "to give Congress the power 'by general laws' to 'prescribe the *effect*,' *i.e.*, the legal effects and consequences, in other states of the 'public acts, records and judicial proceedings' of a state—including, therefore, *legislative acts* as well *judgments* and all other *records and judicial proceedings*.[29]

Congressional action under the Clause has been minimal, "[i]ndeed, there are few clauses of the Constitution, the merely literal possibilities of which have been so little developed as the full faith and credit clause."[30] Only on five occasions has Congress enacted legislation to require States to give full faith and credit to certain types of acts, records, and proceedings. Three of the enactments pertain to family law concerns.

In 1790, the First Congress laid down the rules for authentication of "public acts, records and proceedings" in order to implement the clause and required all courts to give the same effect to the "Acts of the Legislature of Any State" "as they have by law or usage in the courts of such state .. . from which they are taken."[31] Some read this language as meaning that unless Congress prescribes otherwise, a state which prohibits same-sex marriage would nonetheless be required to recognize as valid a same-sex marriage entered into in another state between two of its residents. In 1804, the Eighth Congress extended the

---

[28] See, Cooke, Walter Wheeler, *The Powers of Congress under the Full Faith and Credit Clause*, 28 Yale L. J. 421 (1919).

[29] Cooke, Walter Wheeler, *The Powers of Congress under the Full Faith and Credit Clause*, 28 Yale L. J. 421, 426 (1919) (emphasis added).

[30] *The Constitution of the United States of America Annotated*, Doc. No. 99-16,99th Cong. 1st Sess. at 870 (1987).

[31] "That the acts of the Legislatures of the several states shall be authenticated by having the seal of their respective states affixed thereto; That the records and judicial proceedings of the courts of any state, shall be proved or admitted in any other court within the United States, by the attestation of the clerk, and the seal of the court annexed, if there be a seal, together with a certificate of the judge, chief justice, or presiding magistrate, as the case may be, that the said attestation is in due form. And the said records and judicial proceedings authenticated as aforesaid, shall have such faith and credit given to them in every court within the United States, as they have by law or usage in the courts of the state from whence the said records are or shall be taken."

Act of May 26, 1790, ch. 11, 1 Stat, 122, codified at 28 U.S.C. § 1738.

provisions of the Act of 1790 to State public office books and records; and to the public acts, records, office books, judicial proceedings, courts and offices of the Territories of the United States and countries subject to the jurisdiction of the United States.[32]

In 1980, the 96th Congress enacted the Parental Kidnapping Prevention Act of 1980 ("PKPA"),[33] requiring each State to enforce child custody determinations made by the child's home State. It established the PKPA to promote cooperation between State courts to ensure that a determination of custody and visitation is rendered hi the State which can best decide the interest of the child, and to deter interstate abductions and removals of children. The PKPA requires States to give full faith and credit to sister State child custody decrees unless the State asked to modify the original order has jurisdiction to do so, and the State which issued the original order no longer has jurisdiction or has declined to exercise it. The Justice Department supported Congress' enactment of the PKPA as a valid exercise of its power under the Commerce Clause.[34]

In 1994, the 103rd Congress passed the Full Faith and Credit for Child Support Orders Act,[35] requiring each State to enforce child support orders issued by the child's home State if done consistent with the Act's provisions. The law was designed so that a person who has a valid child support order in one State does not have to obtain a second order in another State should the debtor parent move from the issuing court's jurisdiction. Rather, the second State must recognize the first State's order as valid, but can modify it only when the child and the custodial parent have moved to the State where the modification is sought or have agreed to the modification. Retroactive modification is prohibited, and prospective modification is authorized if the court finds that circumstances exist which justify a change.[36]

Also in 1994, Congress passed the Safe Homes for Women Act of 1994,[37] requiring States to recognize domestic violence protection orders issued by sister States. Any protection order issued by one State or tribe shall be treated and enforced as if it were an order of the enforcing State. The Act extends to

---

[32] 2 Stat. 298 (1804), codified at 28 U.S.C. § 1738.

[33] Pub. L. No. 96-611, 94 Stat. 3569, codified at 28 U.S.C. § 1738A.

[34] See, *Thompson u. Thompson,* 798 F.2d 1547, 1557 (9th Cir. 1986), affirmed by *Thompson v. Thompson,* 484 U.S. 174 (1988) (the Court held that the PKPA did not create an implied cause of action in federal court to determine which of two conflicting custody decrees is valid).

[35] Pub. L. No. 96-611, 94 Stat. 3569, codified at 28 U.S.C. § 1738A.

[36] 42 U.S.C. § 666(a).

[37] Pub. L. No. 103-322, title IV, § 40221(a), 108 Stat. 1930, codified at 18 U.S.C. § 2265.

permanent, temporary, and ex parte protection orders. Full faith and credit is afforded during the period of time in which the order remains valid in the issuing State. Protection orders are only afforded full faith and credit if the due process requirements of the issuing State were met.

In the previous three instances, Congress' exercise of its full faith and credit enforcement power was necessitated by the failure of sister State courts to give full faith and credit to orders not regarded as final judgments. Congress directed sister States to give full faith and credit to child custody, child support, and protection orders from other States. In effect, Congress required each State to give the child custody, child support, and protection orders of other States the same faith and credit it gives its own such orders. The Defense of Marriage Act ("DOMA") differs in one critical aspect from the legislative enactments passed by Congress under its full faith and credit power: the DOMA permits sister States to give no effect to the laws of other States. This is a novel approach to legislating under Congress' full faith and credit enforcement power. The constitutionality of this approach depends in large part upon the scope of Congress' enforcement power under the second sentence of the full faith and credit clause. The issue is whether the authority of Congress "to prescribe the effect" of marriage extends to this type of legislation.

The Supreme Court has never confronted this issue squarely. The Court has, however, recognized continuously that Congress has the power to declare the effect that acts, records, and judicial proceedings of States have in sister States. In 1988 in *Sun Oil v. Wortman*,[38] the Court held that Congress can declare the "effect" under the second sentence of the Clause. Also in 1988, in *Thompson v. Thompson*,[39] the Court upheld another effects clause enactment, the Parental Kidnapping Prevention Act. In other cases the Court has affirmed the position that Congress can prescribe the extrastate effect of acts, records, and proceedings.[40] Although the Court has acknowledged Congress' enforcement power in this regard, it has not defined the scope of the power.

Proponents of the legislation contend that it is a legitimate exercise of Congress' power under the full faith and credit clause to prescribe by general laws the "effect" of same-sex marriages in other States. Opponents of the DOMA counter that the scope of Congress' power does not extend to Congress directing that a State may choose *not* to give any effect to the act of another State. A leading constitutional law scholar argues that "the Constitution delegates to the

---

[38] 486 U.S. 717, 729 (1988).
[39] 484 U.S. 174, 182-83 (1988).
[40] *Mills v. Duryee*, 7 Cranch 481, 11 U.S. 481 (1813); *Pacific Employers Insur. Co. v. Industrial Accident Comm'n.*, 306 U.S. 493, 502 (1939).

United States no power to create categorical exceptions to the Full Faith and Credit Clause. To be sure, the clause does empower Congress to enact general laws to 'prescribe the manner in which such acts, records, and proceedings shall be proved, and the effect thereof.' But that is a far cry from power to decree that official State acts offensive to a majority in Congress need not even be recognized by States that happen to share Congress' view."[41]

EQUAL PROTECTION

On May 20, 1996 in *Romer v. Colorado*,[42] the Supreme Court in a 6-3 opinion struck down as a violation of the Equal Protection Clause of the Fourteenth Amendment[43] an amendment to the Colorado constitution approved by voters, known as Amendment 2, that repealed existing civil rights protections for gays and lesbians in the areas of public accommodations, housing, real estate, insurance, health and welfare, private education, and employment; and prohibited future enactment of anti-discrimination laws protecting gays and lesbians. Justice Kennedy, writing for the majority, said that the Amendment "is a status based enactment divorced from any factual context from which we could discern a relationship to legitimate State interests; it is a classification of persons undertaken for its own sake, something the Equal Protection Clause does not permit." The Court found that the Amendment imposed a special disability upon homosexuals alone by denying them protections taken for granted by most people, and rejected the argument that Amendment 2 only deprived homosexuals of special rights. The Court concluded that Amendment 2 was both too narrowly and too broadly drawn. It was too narrowly drawn because it placed homosexuals in a "solitary class" and singled them out for discriminatory treatment, and it was too broadly drawn because it denies them protections across the board. As justification for the amendment the State said that its purpose was to respect the freedom of association rights of other citizens (such as landlords and employers) who have objections to homosexuality and to serve the State's interest in conserving resources to fight discrimination against other protected groups. Justice Kennedy rejected both of the offered rationales, and concluded that no other plausible basis for Amendment 2 existed other than "animus" towards lesbians and gays.

---

[41] Tribe, Laurence H-, "Toward A Less Perfect Union", New York Times, May 26, 1996.

[42] — S. Ct. — , 64 U.S.L.W. 4353 (May 20, 1996).

[43] The Fourteenth Amendment provides in part: "No state shall. ... deny to any person within its jurisdiction the equal protection of the laws."

An application *of Romer* to DOMA raises the question of whether DOMA creates a legitimate legislative classification that can withstand constitutional scrutiny. Basically *Romer* appears to stand for the proposition that legislation targeting gays and lesbians is constitutionally impermissible under the Equal Protection clause unless the legislative classification bears a rational relationship to a legitimate State purpose. In *Romer,* no rational relationship was found between Amendment 2's targeting of homosexuals and the State's articulated purposes.

DOMA was drafted in response to the possibility that Hawaii will legalize same-sex marriage, and that as a result other States would be forced to recognize such unions under the Full Faith and Credit Clause. Because same-sex marriages are singled out for differential treatment in the bill, DOMA would appear to create a legislative classification for equal protection purposes that must meet a rational relationship test. DOMA seems similar to the legislative classification in Amendment 2 which "imposes a special disability upon those [homosexual] persons alone. Homosexuals are forbidden the safeguards that others may enjoy or seek without constraint." The possibility exists that courts may find that DOMA is not based upon animus towards gays and lesbians because Congress is not prohibiting States from recognizing same-sex marriages.

At this point in time, there is a great deal of uncertainty regarding the implications of the *Romer* decision. For example, it is unclear whether the Court has essentially elevated homosexuals to the level of a 'suspect class' for which no law targeting them can survive or whether Amendment 2*s reach was so broad as to preclude the finding of any rational basis or legitimate State purpose. As a result, it is difficult to say with certainty whether DOMA will survive constitutional scrutiny under *Romer ,* but it is possible to conclude that legislation based upon an animus towards gays and lesbians will be found to be constitutionally suspect. Courts may find a rational basis for DOMA based upon Congress* desire to assist State's in effectuating their domestic relations laws.

In all likelihood, the constitutional parameters of *Romer* will probably not be settled without litigation over time. The Department of Justice has written that "[a]s stated by the President's spokesman Michael MeCurry on Wednesday, May^ 22, the Supreme Court's ruling in *Romer* v. *Evans* does not affect the Department's analysis (that H.R. 3396 is constitutionally sustainable), and the President "would sign the bill if it was presented to him as currently written."[44]

---

[44] Letter from Andrew Fois, Assistant Attorney General, U.S. Dep't of Justice to the Honorable Charles T. Canady, Chairman, House Judiciary Subcommittee (May 29, 1996).

TENTH AMENDMENT

Congress has no express constitutional authority to legislate in the field of domestic relations which includes such matters as marriage and divorce. "Without exception, domestic relations has been a matter of state, not federal, concern and control since the founding of the Republic."[45] The Tenth Amendment provides:

> The powers not delegated to the United States by the Constitution, nor prohibited by it to the States, are reserved to the States respectively, or to the people."

Based upon the Tenth Amendment, the States have the primary authority to regulate marriage, and to control the incidents of marriage provided by State law. As a result, the family law of the fifty States is unquestionably diverse (minimum marriage ages, waiting periods for entering a new marriage following divorce, recognition of common law marriages,[46] and the grounds for terminating marriage). As summarized by the Supreme Court "[i]nsofar as marriage is within temporal control, the States lay on the guiding hand. The whole subject of the domestic relations of husband and wife, parent and child, belongs to the laws of the States and not to the laws of the United States."[47]

Currently, federal law does not define the terms 'marriage' and 'spouse." However, throughout federal law in statutes, rules, regulations, and policies, both terms are frequently used and relied upon for purposes of determining eligibility for federal benefits. Traditionally, the relevant State law definition of marriage or spouse has been adopted. As stated, DOMA defines for federal purposes the words 'marriage' and 'spouse' as applying exclusively to persons of different sex. This change may affect many federal programs and areas, including for example bankruptcy, civil service retirement, armed forces, old-age survivor's benefits, immigration, estate and gift taxes, income taxation, employee benefits rights, social security, veteran's benefits, former spouses annuities, evidentiary privileges, and workmen's compensation.

A criticism that has been leveled at DOMA is that by defining the terms 'marriage' and 'spouse' for purposes of federal law, Congress is impermissibly

---

[45] *Aukenbrandt v. Richards,* 112 S. Ct. 2206 (1992).

[46] Thirteen states and the District of Columbia continue to recognize common law marriage. (Alabama, Colorado, District of Columbia, Georgia, Idaho, Iowa, Kansas, Montana, Ohio, Oklahoma, Pennsylvania, Rhode Island, South Carolina, Texas).

[47] *Hisquierdo y. Hisquierdo,* 439 U.S. 572, 581 (1979)

intruding into an area traditionally regulated by and reserved to the States under the Tenth Amendment. Some have argued though that the Tenth Amendment does not present a bar to Congressional involvement in this case because the Constitution clearly delegates to Congress under the Full Faith and Credit Clause the power to enforce the Clause. Furthermore, DOMA purports to define these terms only for determining the meaning of federal law and rules and regulations of federal agencies. Moreover, under the Full Faith and Credit Clause when Congress has exercised it power in the past, many of the legislative enactments have addressed domestic relations concerns.

CONCLUSION

The States currently possess the authority to decide whether to recognize an out-of-state marriage, regardless of whether it is a different-sex or same-sex marriage. The Full Faith and Credit Clause has rarely been used by States to validate marriages because marriages are not "legal judgments." The Full Faith and Credit Clause applies principally to the interstate recognition and enforcement of judgments. With respect to cases decided under the Full Faith and Credit Clause that involve conflicting State statutes, the Supreme Court examines the significant aggregation of contacts the forum has with the parties and the occurrence or transaction to decide which State's law to apply. Similarly, based upon generally accepted legal principles, the States routinely decide whether a marriage contracted in another State will be recognized in-State by examining whether it has a significant relationship with the spouses and the marriage. Because States possess authority to decide whether to recognize an out-of-state marriage, it appears that there is little legal necessity for section 2 the Defense of Marriage Act which would allow States to deny legal recognition to same-sex marriages contracted out-of-state.

The Congress is empowered under the Full Faith and Credit Clause of the Constitution to prescribe the manner that public acts, commonly understood to mean legislative acts, records, and proceedings shall be proved and the effect of such acts, records, and proceedings in other States. Only on five occasions has Congress enacted legislation based upon this power. It required States to implement the Clause by giving full faith and credit to certain types of acts, records, and proceedings. Three of the Congressional enactments in this regard pertained to modifiable family law orders (child custody, child support, and domestic protection) that were not final judgments which necessitated Congressional involvement in order to afford them interstate recognition. Because Congress has express constitutional power to enforce the Full Faith and Credit Clause some have argued that the Tenth Amendment is inapplicable to the Defense of Marriage Act because the power to implement full faith and credit has been delegated to the Congress not the States. Others contend that Congress is legislating on a substantive marriage issue that is properly and traditionally within the province of the States.

The Supreme Court's recent decision in *Romer v. Colorado*,[48] regarding the equal protection rights of gays and lesbians, presents different issues concerning the constitutionality of the Defense of Marriage Act. Basically *Romer* appears to stand for the proposition that legislation targeting gays and lesbians is constitutionally impermissible under the Equal Protection clause unless the legislative classification bears a rational relationship to a legitimate State purpose. Because same-sex marriages are singled out for differential treatment, DOMA appears to create a legislative classification for equal protection purposes that must meet a rational relationship test. At this point in time because there is a great deal of uncertainty regarding the implications of the *Romer* decision, it is difficult to say with certainty whether DOMA will survive constitutional scrutiny under *Romer. It* is possible to conclude, however, that based upon the *Romer* decision legislation based upon an animus towards gays and lesbians will be found to be constitutionally suspect. Courts may find that DOMA is not based upon animus towards gays and lesbians because Congress is not prohibiting States from recognizing same-sex marriages if they so choose.

---

[48] __ S. Ct __ 64 U.S.L.W. 4363 (May 20, 1996).

Chapter 2

DEFENSE OF MARRIAGE ACT[*]

Mark Eddy

INTRODUCTION

Legislation that would prohibit federal recognition of same-sex marriages and allow individual states to refuse to recognize such marriages performed in other states was considered and approved by the 104th Congress. Called the Defense of Marriage Act, the measure responds to a court case in Hawaii that could result in the legalization there of marriages between two persons of the same sex. President Clinton signed the measure into law on September 21,1996 (P.L. 104-199).

THE SITUATION IN HAWAII

In May 1991, three same-sex couples filed a lawsuit against the State of Hawaii to contest a marriage law that prohibits them from obtaining marriage licenses. The complaint alleged a violation of the couples' right to privacy and equal protection under the Hawaii State Constitution. The trial court dismissed the case, which was appealed to the Supreme Court of Hawaii.

---

[*] Excerpted from CRS Report 96-589 GOV.

On May 5, 1993, the Hawaii Supreme Court reversed the trial court and remanded the case back for trial.[1] Although the Supreme Court found that there is no fundamental right to same-sex marriage under the right to privacy, the court did conclude that the marriage law does deny the same-sex couples equal protection rights in violation of article I, Section 5 of the Hawaii Constitution.[2] Under the "strict scrutiny" test, the state must show that its marriage statute is justified by compelling state interests and is narrowly drawn to avoid unnecessary abridgments of the applicant couples' constitutional rights.

The Hawaii Legislature created a Commission on Sexual Orientation and the Law to study the matter. In its 316-page report issued in December 1995, the Commission identified four basic policy reasons why the right to legally marry should be extended to same-sex couples: (1) the denial of the right to marry is a denial of the state and federal constitutional right to equal protection of the law; (2) the Hawaii Supreme Court's requirement in the *Baehr* case that the state show a compelling state interest for the denial and the reasons advanced by those who support the denial show a close parallel to the landmark case *of Loving* v. *Virginia,* 388 U.S. 1 (1967), in which the U.S. Supreme Court found unconstitutional a Virginia statute outlawing interracial marriage; (3) the argument that same-sex marriage should he barred because it would not lead to procreation is invalid, inconsistent, and discriminatory because this standard is not applied to heterosexual marriage; and (4) the religious beliefs of those who would ban such marriages can certainly be adhered to by those persons .or their churches but they cannot be imposed by state law on others who do not subscribe to such beliefs.[3]

The remanded trial was held in September 1996, and was decided in favor of the plaintiffs on December 3, 1996.[4] Given the likelihood of appeal, however, the issue in Hawaii is not expected to be settled until at least the end of 1997. In response to the case in Hawaii, at least 36 other state legislatures have moved to forbid same-sex marriages within their own jurisdictions, and such measures have been enacted in 16 states (including Hawaii). A related bill was considered and passed by the 104th Congress, as discussed below.

---

[1] *Baehr v. Lewin,* 852 P.2d 44 (Haw. 1993).

[2] Right to Equal Protection, Article 1, Section 5 of the Hawaii Constitution provides: "No person shall be deprived of life, liberty or property without due process of law, nor be denied the equal protection of the laws, nor be denied the enjoyment of the person's civil rights or be discriminated against in the exercise thereof because of race, religion, sex or ancestry."

[3] *Report of the Commission on Sexual Orientation and the Law,* Thomas P. Gill, Chair, December 8, 1995, p. iii.

[4] The full text of the decision can be found on the Internet at http://sterbuUetin.com/today/news/ssruling.txt.

THE DEFENSE OF MARRIAGE ACT

The Defense of Marriage Act (DOMA) was introduced in the House by Representatives Barr and Largent on May 7,1996, as H.R. 3396, and in the Senate by Senators Nickles and Dole on the following day as S. 1740.[5] The House bill was referred to the House Judiciary Subcommittee on the Constitution, which held hearings on May 15,1996. The subcommittee held a mark-up session, on May 30, at which the bill was approved 8-4 on a party-line vote and was forwarded without amendment to the full committee. The full committee considered the bill June 11-12, and ordered it reported as introduced by a vote of 20-10 (H.Rept. 104-664). The House approved the measure, unamended, by a vote of 342-67 on July 12, 1996.[6] The Senate bill was referred to the Committee on the Judiciary, where hearings were held on July 11 and where there was an effort to attach the Employment Non-Discrimination Act (S. 932) to DOMA as an amendment.[7] On September 10,1996, H.R. 3396 was laid before the Senate by unanimous consent, and the bill was passed, unamended, by a vote of 85-14.[8] President Clinton signed the measure into law without ceremony on September 21, 1996 (P.L. 104-199).

DOMA seeks "[t]o define and protect the institution of marriage" by amending the U.S. Code in two places. First, it amends Chapter 115 of title 28 by adding Section 1738C, which states:

No State, territory, or possession of the United States, or Indian tribe, shall be required to give effect to any public act, record, or judicial proceeding of any other State, territory, possession, or tribe respecting a relationship between persons of the same sex that is treated as a marriage under the laws of such other State, territory, possession, or tribe, or a right or claim arising from such relationship.

Second, it amends Chapter 1 of Title 1 by adding at the end the following:

[5] *Congressional Record,* Daily Edition, v. 142, May 7,1996. p. H45Q2; Ibid., May 8, 1996. p. S4869.

[6] Ibid, July 11, 1996, p. H7270-80 and H7441-49; Ibid., July 12, 1996, p. H7480-H7506.

[7] For background on the Employment Non-Discrimination Act see: U.S. Library of Congress. Congressional Research Service. *Sexual Orientation Discrimination in Employment: Legislation and Issues in the 104th Congress.* CRS Report 94-592 GOV, by Mark Eddy. Washington, 1996.

[8] *Congressional Record,* Daily Edition, v. 142, September 10, 1996, p. S10100-129.

In determining the meaning of any Act of Congress, or of any ruling, regulation, or interpretation of the various administrative bureaus and agencies of the United States, the word 'marriage' means only a legal union between one man and one woman as husband and wife, and the word 'spouse' refers only to a person of the opposite sex who is a husband or a wife.

In proposing these two amendments to the *U.S. Code,* this short bill proved contentious in the congressional hearings, markup sessions, and floor debate, as well as in media coverage of the issue. Marriage is both a religious and a civil institution. Some religious denominations perform same-sex marriages and recognize same-sex unions, although most do not. DOMA, of course, is concerned only with civil marriage, as are the major arguments for and against DOMA that are summarized below, as paraphrased from hearings testimony and the media.[9]

PRO-CON ANALYSIS

The Institution of Marriage Needs the Protection of DOMA

Pro

Homosexual marriage, which is against natural law, would abolish thousands of years of cultural and legal tradition and could lead to the dismantling of Western civilization by destroying the family. Marriage exists mainly for the begetting and raising of children, which homosexuals cannot do. Same-sex marriage is the greatest threat to the family that homosexual activists have concocted. It would cause the heterosexual family to lose its special legal, social, and economic status. The sanctity of the marriage bond has already been cheapened and weakened by no-fault divorce, out-of-wedlock pregnancies, and sexual promiscuity. Homosexual activists now feel emboldened to deal the final injury — advancing the separation of the two sexes from each other in marriage. The need is not to stretch the institution further out of

---

[9] See, for example: Holly Idelson. "GOP Sets Pre-Emptive Strike on Same-Sex Marriages." *Congressional Quarterly,* v. 54, May 18,1996. p. 1393; Anne Underwood and Bruce Shenitz. "Do You, Tom, Take Harry..." *Newsweek,* v. 126, December 11,1995, p. 82; Thomas Stoddard and Bruce Fein. "Gay Marriage: Should Homosexual Marriages Be Recognized Legally?" *American Bar Association Journal,* v. 76, January 1990. p. 42; Andrew Sullivan, "The Politics of Homosexuality." *New Republic,* v. 208, May 10, 1993. p. 24; Hadley Arkes. "The Closet Straight." *National Review,* v. 45, July 5, 1993. p. 43.

shape but to reassert support for the only model that really works: family based on a union between a man and a woman.

Con

By seeking to marry, gays and lesbians are showing their belief and faith in the institution of marriage, their desire to strengthen it, not weaken it. To suggest that homosexual couples threaten to undermine the stability of heterosexual marriages is absurd. Heterosexual couples will continue to predominate even if gay people gain the right to marry. If two men or two women fall in love and want to marry, it in no way detracts from a man and a woman who are in love and want to marry. Love is not a limited resource, a zero-sum game. Nor will there be a shortage of marriage licenses if same-sex couples can wed. Marriage is not a limited commodity. When same-sex couples gain the right to marry, they will not "use up" or "harm" marriage, nor will they take anything away from opposite-sex married couples. Marriage and all its privileges and responsibilities will remain fully available for everyone. Civil marriage is not just for the conceiving and raising of children. Many heterosexual couples are childless, and many gay couples are raising children. All children deserve the stability and protection of the family structure. There is no objective justification for continuing the ban on same-sex marriages.

Marriage is By Definition between a Man and a Woman

Pro

Marriage constitutes the bringing together of the two sexes. Homosexual relationships do not offer the richness and complementarity that men and women find in marriage and family life. A man and a woman must be present in a marriage. To enter marriage, couples must meet its qualifications. Any attempt to rewrite the rules that everyone else must observe is an attempt to have special rights, not equal rights. Eliminating an entire sex from the picture and then calling it marriage is not a mere expansion of an institution, but rather the destruction of a principle. If we abandon our fundamental definition of marriage, other sexual preferences such as polygamy, pederasty, incest, and bestiality will also seek governmental validation. Once the one-man, one-woman definition is abandoned, there is no logical reason to limit marriage to two people (or even to people).

Con

To allow gay and lesbian couples to enter into the institution of marriage would not redefine marriage but would extend this basic human right to a currently disfranchised group, as has occurred in the past. African American slaves were not allowed to marry. Asian Americans were not allowed to marry in some Western states. Until recently, marriage was by definition between two people of the same race. Persons who previously opposed extending the right to marry to these groups used the same arguments as are now being used to oppose same-sex marriages. The legal institution of marriage has historically been used to deny groups their full rights as citizens, and continues to be so used in the case of gays and lesbians.

The Measure is Constitutional[10]

Pro

The U.S. Constitution grants Congress the right to legislate as to the effect of the Full Faith and Credit Clause.[11] Congress has legislated before with respect to full faith and credit, and that is what Congress is doing again with DOMA. All this legislation does is to let each state decide the issue of same-sex marriage for itself, as is provided for under the court-sanctioned public policy exception to full faith and credit, whereby a state is not required to apply another state's laws in violation of its own legitimate public policy. Equal protection issues are not raised by DOMA because the Supreme Court affirmed in *Bowers* v. *Hardwick,* 478 U.S. 186 (1986), that there is no constitutionally guaranteed right to sodomy. Moreover, the Justice Department's Office of Legislative Affairs stated, in two letters to the House Judiciary Committee, that it believed that H.R. 3396 would be sustained as constitutional and that the bill did not raise any legal issues that necessitated further comment by the Department.

---

[10] For a legal discussion of DOMA, see: U.S. Library of Congress. Congressional Research Service. *Interstate Marriage Recognition and the Defense of Marriage Act.* CRS Report 96-529 A, by Gina Marie Stevens. Washington, 1996.

[11] Article IV, Section 1 of the U.S. Constitution states: "Full Faith and Credit shall be given in each State to the public Acts, Records and judicial Proceedings of every other State. And the Congress may by general Laws prescribe the Manner in which such Acts, Records and Proceedings shall be proved, and the Effect thereof."

Con

At best, DOMA is unnecessary because the states already have the power to refuse to honor same-sex marriages conducted in other states under the public policy exemption to the Full Faith and Credit Clause. At worst, it is flagrantly unconstitutional. There is no constitutional authority for Congress to limit fall faith and credit between the states or to define the institution of marriage at the federal level. It is true that Congress has legislated before with respect to full faith and credit, but in each case Congress acted to promote uniformity or increase the credit' that states must give to other states' acts above what was otherwise constitutionally required. In this case Congress is acting to decrease the full faith and credit obligation. There is no precedent for Congress inviting some states to disregard the official acts of others. Moreover, DOMA is based on anti-gay disapproval, dislike, or discomfort, the very animus recently rejected by the Supreme Court as a basis for government discrimination in *Romer* v. *Colorado,* 116 S.Ct. 1620 (1996), which affirmed the equal protection rights of gay and lesbian Americans.

Federal Legislation on Marriage is Appropriate

Pro

It is necessary for Congress to define marriage in federal law because homosexuals are thwarting the will of the people through judicial activism. Three judges hi Hawaii should not be permitted to redefine marriage not only for the people of Hawaii but for the rest of the country as well. DOMA ensures that each state can do as it wants free of any constitutional requirement that might arise under the Full Faith and Credit Clause of the U.S. Constitution. DOMA does not prevent homosexual marriage at the state level; it only defines marriage for federal purposes. It allows each state to establish its own public policy on homosexual marriage. DOMA is necessary to define federal benefits, rights, and privileges for married persons uniformly throughout the country. Without DOMA, the federal government would have to acknowledge same-sex marriages performed in Hawaii or elsewhere. DOMA thus eliminates legal uncertainly concerning federal benefits.

Con

Family law has always been the province of the states, not the federal government, and should remain so. It is not necessary for Congress now to speak on marriage after more than 200 years of silence. Americans do not want more federal intrusion in their personal lives. If same-sex unions were to be approved by a state, DOMA would have the effect of unjustly treating these legally married couples as strangers under all federal laws and programs, from Medicaid through the tax code. Same-sex marriages are not now legal anywhere in the United States, and the earliest any change could happen is toward the end of 1997, when the final appeal to the Hawaii Supreme Court will likely he decided. There was no need to rush this bill through Congress before the issue was fully debated and considered by the American people. DOMA was a cynical election-year tactic to divide Americans and bolster Republican prospects to retain a majority in Congress. Under the Republican leadership in Congress, the House and Senate Judiciary Committees, the very committees charged with protecting the civil rights of all Americans, are now promoting intolerance.

Homosexuals Should Not Be Allowed to Marry

Pro

Homosexuals are not deserving of special rights such as the right to marry. Homosexuals enjoy the basic rights of citizenship — they can vote, own property, hold jobs — but they cannot claim special treatment beyond those rights. Homosexuality is not immutable, like race, but is behaviorally based. If government begins granting rights based on behavior, there is no logical stopping point. Smokers, gamblers, pornographers, sex addicts, pofygamists, and pedophiles could all claim rights to protection against discrimination. The state should not encourage unhealthy behavior by granting special benefits for it. Nor should taxpayers be expected to pay the economic costs of same-sex marriages, such as family health benefits and survivors benefits. In any case, the rights and protections granted by marriage can be achieved by other legal means. Homosexuals can draft wills to leave their property to their partners, medical powers of attorney to ensure hospital visitation rights, and contractual agreements to govern distribution of assets in the event of a breakup. Domestic partner benefits are granted by many employers. What homosexuals really seek are not the rights and privileges of marriage but full acceptance by society of their lifestyle. Validation of homosexual relationships, however, would present a fundamental danger to the structure, moral fiber, and future of American society and should not be granted.

Con

This legislation sends the message that it is acceptable to discriminate against gay persons. The American values of freedom and diversity require that we extend the same rights to lesbian and gay unions that are accorded heterosexual unions. It is in society's interest to encourage long-term, stable relationships among all its citizens, including its lesbian and gay citizens. Many lesbians and gays are raising children, and their children also deserve the rights, benefits, and protections that marriage affords. Without the right to marry, lesbian and gay couples can be refused hospital visitation rights, health coverage and other forms of insurance, inheritance and taxation rights, government benefits for spouses, immigration rights for spouses, and other rights heterosexuals take for granted. It is true that some same-sex couples prepare legal documents to govern inheritance, child visitation rights, and other issues in the event of death or a breakup, but such pacts are not necessarily honored by judges and can be challenged by others. Civil marriage rights would allow judges to apply the same divorce laws to same-sex couples that now apply only to heterosexual couples. Just as the state should not interfere in any way with religious ceremonies, religious groups should not govern who gets a civil marriage license. Lesbians and gays are not seeking active approval — people are entitled to their private beliefs — but equal protection under the law as guaranteed by the U.S. Constitution.

Chapter 3

THE DEFENSE OF MARRIAGE ACT: FEDERAL LAWS IN WHICH BENEFITS, RIGHTS AND PRIVILEGES ARE CONTINGENT ON MARITAL STATUS[*]

Barry R. Bedrick

The Defense of Marriage Act,[1] which became law on September 21 1996, defines "marriage" as "a legal union between one man and one woman as husband and wife"; similarly it defines "spouse" as referring "only to a person of the opposite sex who is a husband or a wife." Because the Act makes both definitions apply "[i]n determining the meaning of any Act of Congress," it potentially affects the interpretation of a wide variety of federal laws in which marital status is a factor.

In connection with the enactment of the Defense of Marriage Act, we identify federal laws in which benefits, rights, and privileges are contingent on marital status. We identify more generally all those laws in the United States Code in which marital status is a factor, even though some of these laws may not directly create benefits, rights, or privileges.

---

[*] Excerpted from General Accounting Office (GAO) Report # GAO/OGC-97-16 Defense of Marriage Act.
[1] Public Law 104-199, 110 Stat. 2419.

To find laws that meet these criteria, we conducted searches for various words or word stems ("marr," "spouse," "widow," etc.), chosen to elicit marital status, in several electronic databases that contain the text of federal laws. From the collection of laws in the United States Code that we found through those searches, we eliminated (1) laws that included one or more of our search terms but that were not relevant to your request[2] and (2) as agreed with your staff, any laws enacted after the Defense of Marriage Act. The result is a collection of 1049 federal laws classified to the United States Code in which marital status is a factor.

This collection of laws is as complete and representative as can be produced by a global electronic search of the kind we conducted, but such a search has several limitations. Most significantly, it cannot capture every individual law in the United States Code in which marital status figures. However, we believe that the probability is high that it has identified those *programs* in the Code in which marital status is a factor.

Because of the inherent limitations of any computer search[3] and the many ways in which the laws in the United States Code may have dealt with marital status, the only way to create an exhaustive list of laws in the Code implicating marital status would be to read and analyze the Code in its entirety. We believe that such an effort would not generate substantially more useful information than we have provided here.

A second caveat concerning our data is that they include only laws classified to the United States Code. As you know, the Code is a compendium of "general and permanent" laws. Although appropriations and annual authorizations, for example, might contain references to marital status, they are typically in effect for a single year, and therefore do not appear in the Code.

Finally, no conclusions can be drawn, from our identification of a law as one in which marital status is a factor, concerning the effect of the law on married people versus single people. A particular law may create either

---

[2] For example, our search for the word stem "marr," designed to capture words such as "marriage" and "marry," also produced references to laws mentioning bone marrow transplants, the city of Marrakesh, and proper names containing the letters "marr."

[3] One such limitation results from the use of statutory definitions. Our search for occurrences of "spouse" would find a law defining "relative," for purposes of a program, as including a spouse. It would not find the laws in that program that, by referring to "relative," apply to a spouse. A search for "relative" does not solve this problem. That word is used commonly in senses unrelated to marital status (as are other terms such as "single"). A computer cannot distinguish between these senses; a lawyer would have to examine each occurrence of "relative" to determine whether it refers to marital status.

advantages or disadvantages for those who are married, or may apply to both married and single people. For example, those who are unmarried fare better than their married counterparts under the so-called marriage penalty provisions of the tax laws, while married couples enjoy estate tax benefits not available to the unmarried. Other laws apply both to married and single people by virtue of terms like "survivors," "relatives," "family," and "household."

The raw data produced by our searches were in a form that made them unwieldy and difficult to use. One reason for this is the sheer number of individual laws that we identified. Also, we conducted multiple searches in several databases, resulting in several separate lists in varying formats. Finally, the laws on the lists were organized as they are in the United States Code; for a reader attempting to understand what kinds of laws make marital status a factor, that organization is not consistently helpful. Some of the Code's 50 titles contain laws on seemingly unrelated subjects. Title 42, under the broad designation "The Public Health and Welfare," includes laws ranging from Social Security to nuclear waste disposal to civil rights and privacy protection. Conversely, closely parallel provisions may appear in different titles: benefits for most federal civil servants are in Title 5, Government Organization and Employees, but similar provisions for Foreign Service officers are in Title 22, Foreign Relations and Intercourse.

To give readers a sense of the kinds of federal laws in which marital status is a factor, we classified the laws on the list into the following 13 categories:[4]

❑ Social Security and Related Programs, Housing, and Food Stamps
❑ Veterans' Benefits
❑ Taxation
❑ Federal Civilian and Military Service Benefits
❑ Employment Benefits and Related Laws
❑ Immigration, Naturalization, and Aliens
❑ Indians
❑ Trade, Commerce, and Intellectual Property
❑ Financial Disclosure and Conflict of Interest
❑ Crimes and Family Violence
❑ Loans, Guarantees, and Payments in Agriculture

---

[4] The order of the categories is not significant, except that the first four are those in which marital status is most pervasive, and are the largest.

❑   Federal Natural Resources and Related Laws
❑   Miscellaneous Laws

While we believe this classification scheme is useful for organizing the hundreds of statutes on the list, and for representing the range of federal programs and activities in which the law makes marital status relevant, it should not be regarded as definitive. Other ways of categorizing these laws would be equally valid. Moreover, the categories we use are not mutually exclusive: many laws could arguably be in a different category. A general description of each category and a few examples of the laws it contains are in the Appendix I.

APPENDIX: CATEGORIES OF LAWS INVOLVING MARITAL STATUS

Category 1—Social Security and Related Programs, Housing, and Food Stamps

This category includes the major federal health and welfare programs, particularly those considered entitlements, such as Social Security retirement and disability benefits, food stamps, welfare, and Medicare and Medicaid.[5] Most of these laws are found in Title 42 of the United States Code, The Public Health and Welfare; food stamp legislation is in Title 7, Agriculture.

In many of these programs, recognition of the marital relationship is integral to the design of the program. For example, the law establishing the Old Age, Survivors, and Disability Insurance (OASDI) program (Social Security) is written in terms of the rights of husbands and wives, and widows and widowers. Once the law sets forth the basic right of an individual participant to retirement benefits, it prescribes in great detail the corresponding rights of the current or former spouse. Whether one is eligible for Social Security payments, and if so how much one receives, are both dependent on marital status. This is reflected in the provisions for what

---

[5] The recently enacted welfare reform bill, the Personal Responsibility and Work Opportunity Reconciliation Act of 1996, greatly affected some of the provisions in this category, but the changes are not generally effective until July 1997. Where both the old and new provisions appear in the United States Code, we have included both—the ones in effect until July 1997 and the ones that take effect thereafter—in Enclosure II (available in GAO report #GAO/OGC-97-16).

happens upon the death of a beneficiary: if certain conditions are met, then a spouse or a divorced spouse (as well as a widow or widower) has a right to payments based on the marriage, rather than on his or her own earnings.

The part of the Social Security Act that governs the OASDI program is unusual in that, unlike many other laws we have identified, it defines the terms "husband" and "wife." It does so in terms of state law: a person is the wife or husband of an insured individual for purposes of OASDI if "the courts of the State [of domicile] ... would find that such applicant and such insured individual were validly married ..." or, if not, that under the state's laws of intestate succession, the person would have the same status with respect to the individual's property as a wife or husband, widow or widower. Those 65 or older who are eligible for Social Security retirement benefits, or who have received Social Security disability benefits for at least 2 years, are also eligible for benefits under Medicare.

The Social Security Act also authorizes the Supplemental Security Income (SSI) program, for the needy aged, blind, and disabled. Under SSI, both the level of income to determine eligibility and the level of benefits for those who are eligible differ, depending whether the applicant has an eligible spouse or not. SSI defines "eligible spouse" as an aged, blind, or disabled individual who is the husband or wife of another aged, blind, or disabled individual. The SSI law goes on to say that, in determining whether two individuals are husband and wife, state law will generally apply, except that if a man and a woman have been determined to be husband and wife for purpose of OASDI or, if a man and woman are found to be holding themselves out to the community as husband and wife, they are also husband and wife for purposes of SSI.

Child support enforcement is another program, also established under the Social Security Act, that contains provisions affecting spouses. Its purpose is to provide help (1) in enforcing the support obligations of absent parents to their children and to the spouse with whom the children may be living, and (2) in obtaining child and spousal support. If an obligation has been established under state law for one spouse to support another, and if the supported spouse is receiving assistance under Medicaid (see below) or AFDC (Aid to Families with Dependent Children), then a state participating in the child support enforcement program must help enforce the support obligation.

Medicaid is a jointly funded federal-state entitlement program to provide medical assistance to qualifying low-income people, including those

34   Barry R. Bedrick

eligible for AFDC[6] and SSI, non-AFDC low-income children and pregnant women, and low-income Medicare beneficiaries. In determining a person's eligibility for Medicaid based on income, states may consider the spouse's financial responsibility for the person, but may not consider anyone else's financial responsibility. Spouses are considered "essential" to individuals receiving Medicaid benefits, and are therefore eligible for medical assistance themselves. The Medicaid statute also prescribes how to account for the income and resources of the spouse of an institutionalized person, for purposes of determining that person's eligibility for benefits.

In the broad federal program of housing assistance for low-income families the definition of "families" takes marital status into account. For some purposes, the term means families whose heads, or their spouses, are elderly, near-elderly, or disabled. However, the same provision includes a definition of families—"2 or more elderly persons, near-elderly persons, or persons with disabilities living together"—that does not require any marital relationship. The same law makes marital status a factor in determining whether a family qualifies for assistance in terms of income. Applicants may exclude $550 for each family member who is under 18, or is disabled or handicapped or a full-time student, but this exclusion does not apply to "the head of the household or his spouse." Also to be excluded is any payment by a member of the family for the support and maintenance of a spouse or former spouse who does not live in the household.

In the National Affordable Housing program, marital status also is significant. The program is intended to assist families, and particularly "first-time homebuyers," in buying homes. "First-time homebuyer" is defined, in part, as an individual "and his or her spouse" who have not owned a home during the preceding 3 years.

In the Food Stamp program (also to be broadly affected by welfare reform), marital status is not central, but does play a role. Eligibility for benefits under the program is determined on the basis of households, and "household" includes not only spouses who live together, but also groups of individuals who live together and customarily buy and prepare food together.

---

[6] Under welfare reform, AFDC will be replaced by Temporary Assistance for Needy Families in July 1997. States will have the option of terminating Medicaid benefits for individuals who refuse to work.

Category 2—Veterans' Benefits

Veterans' benefits, which are codified in Title 38 of the United States Code, include pensions, indemnity compensation for service-connected deaths, medical care, nursing home care, right to burial in veterans' cemeteries, educational assistance, and housing. Husbands or wives of veterans have many rights and privileges by virtue of the marital relationship.

A surviving spouse or child of a veteran is entitled to receive monthly dependency and indemnity compensation payments when the veteran's death was service-connected, and to receive a monthly pension when the veteran's death was not service-connected. If it is discovered that a veteran's marriage is invalid, the purported marriage may nevertheless be deemed valid under certain circumstances, as long as a "real" widow or widower does not ask for benefits.

Veterans who have at least a 30 percent disability are entitled to additional disability compensation if they have dependents. For this purpose a spouse is considered a dependent. A veteran's spouse may also receive compensation if a veteran disappears. On the other hand, a spouse's estate is considered along with the veteran's when the Secretary of Veterans Affairs determines whether it is reasonable that some part of the veteran's assets be used for the veteran's maintenance and whether the Secretary should discontinue paying the pension.

The spouses of certain veterans are entitled to medical care provided by the government. In determining, based on income and assets, whether a veteran has the ability to defray necessary home care and medical expenses, the property of the spouse of the veteran is included as an asset of the veteran. Spouses of veterans may be beneficiaries of National Service Life Insurance, and are also eligible for interment in national cemeteries if the veteran is eligible. The surviving spouse of a veteran who died of a service-connected disability is entitled to educational assistance for up to 45 months, and to job counseling, training, and placement services. Spouses and widows or widowers of certain veterans also enjoy preferences in federal employment.

Category 3—Taxation

The distinction between married and unmarried status is pervasive in federal tax law; this is one of the largest categories, with 179 provisions. Tax law does not define such terms as "husband," "wife," or "married."

Marital status figures in federal tax law in provisions as basic as those giving married taxpayers the option to file joint or separate income tax returns. It is also seen in the related provisions prescribing different tax consequences depending on whether a taxpayer is married filing jointly, married filing separately, unmarried but the head of a household, or unmarried and not the head of a household.

The different treatment in the tax code of married couples and single individuals gives rise to one of the most contentious tax policy issues, the so-called marriage penalty (and its counterpart, the marriage bonus). This issue comes into play in connection with income tax rates, the treatment of capital losses, credits for the elderly and disabled, taxation of Social Security benefits, and a number of other provisions of the tax code. In our report, *Tax Administration: Income Tax Treatment of Married and Single Individuals*,[7] we identified 59 provisions in income tax law under which tax liability depends in part on whether a taxpayer is married or single.

Marital status also plays a key role in the estate and gift tax laws and in the part of the tax code dealing with taxation on the sale of property. For estate tax purposes, property transferred to one spouse as the result of the death of another is deductible for purposes of determining the value of the decedent's estate. Gifts from one spouse to another are deductible for purposes of the gift tax. Gifts from one spouse to a third party are deemed to be from both spouses equally. The law permits transfers of property from one spouse to another (or to a former spouse if the transfer is incident to a divorce) without any recognition of gain or loss for tax purposes. These provisions permit married couples to transfer substantial sums to one another, and to third parties, without tax liability in circumstances in which single people would not enjoy the same privilege.

Category 4—Federal Civilian and Military Service Benefits

This category includes laws dealing with current and retired federal officers and employees, members of the Armed Forces, elected officials, and judges, in which marital status is a factor. Typically these laws address the various health, leave, retirement, survivor, and insurance benefits provided

---

[7] GAO/GGD-96-175, September 3, 1996.

by the United States to those in federal service and their families. Over 270 of the 1049 provisions we found fall in this category. They appear primarily in Title 5 of the United States Code, Government Organization and Employees, for civilian employees, and Title 10, Armed Forces, for military members. However, parallel provisions are found in 19 other titles covering, for example, Foreign Service officers (Title 22, Foreign Relations and Intercourse), Central Intelligence Agency employees (Title 50, War and National Defense), Lighthouse Service employees (Title 33, Navigation and Navigable Waters), and members of the Coast Guard (Title 14, Coast Guard).

Marital status is a factor in these laws in many ways. Among the laws governing federal employees and officers, it figures in the following provisions: a law establishing health benefits or survivor benefits for spouses; a law prescribing the order of precedence in payment of final paychecks and life insurance benefits of employees or officers who die without having designated a beneficiary; and a law determining the rights of current or former spouses to a retirement annuity after the death of an employee.

In addition, under provisions for reimbursement of employees' expenses in connection with a government-ordered relocation, spouses are eligible for per diem allowances or subsistence payments. Federal civil service employees are entitled to unpaid leave in order to care for a spouse with a serious health problem, and an employee disabled by work-related injuries receives augmented compensation if he or she is married.

A different set of laws governs military personnel and their families. Some of the provisions unique to military service include: employment assistance and transitional services for spouses of members being separated from military service; continued commissary privileges for dependents, including spouses, of members separated for spousal or child abuse, and the right of minor spouses of overseas military personnel to free secondary education through the Defense Department school system.

Category 5—Employment Benefits and Related Laws

Marital status comes into play in many different ways in federal laws relating to employment in the private sector. Most such laws appear in Title 29 of the United States Code, Labor. However, others are in Title 30, Mineral Lands and Mining; Title 33, Navigation and Navigable Waters; and

Title 45, Railroads.

This category includes laws that address the rights of employees under employer-sponsored employee benefit plans; that provide for continuation of employer-sponsored health benefits after events like the death or divorce of the employee; and that give employees the right to unpaid leave in order to care for a seriously ill spouse. In addition, Congress has extended special benefits in connection with certain occupations, like mining and public safety. The spouse of a coal miner who dies of black lung disease is entitled to benefits, for example. The surviving spouse of a public safety officer killed in the line of duty is eligible for a death benefit of up to $100,000.

Spouses are sometimes excluded from coverage as employees under certain laws. For example, under the National Labor Relations Act, an individual working for his or her spouse does not come within the definition of "employee," and therefore does not have the right, available under the Act to other employees, to organize or to engage in collective bargaining. If the only regular employees of a business are the owner and his or her spouse, then the business is not subject to regulation of wages and hours under the Fair Labor Standards Act of 1938 (FLSA). Similarly, the spouse or other family member of an employer working in agriculture is not covered under FLSA requirements like minimum wage.

Some laws protect the interests of one spouse when the other becomes eligible for some benefit. The Employee Retirement Income Security Act prohibits an employee from changing beneficiaries in a retirement plan or from waiving the joint and survivor annuity form of retirement benefit, without the written consent of his or her spouse.

The Railroad Retirement Act confers many rights on retired railroad employees and their spouses. Spouses may be eligible for annuities and lump sum benefits. Congress has also enacted a workers' compensation law for longshore and harbor workers that establishes survivor benefits for spouses.

Category 6—Immigration, Naturalization, and Aliens

This category includes laws governing the conditions under which noncitizens may enter and remain in the United States, be deported, or become citizens. Most are found in Title 8, Aliens and Nationality.

The law gives special consideration to spouses of immigrants and aliens in a wide variety of circumstances. Under immigration law, aliens may receive special status by virtue of their employment, and that treatment may extend to their spouses. For example, the spouses of aliens who come to the United States on a temporary basis (to work as registered nurses, seasonal agricultural workers, or in certain specialty occupations), and who meet other criteria, are not subject to the worldwide numerical limitations on levels of immigration. Also, spouses of aliens granted asylum can be given the same status if they accompany or join their spouses.

Spouses of aliens do not enjoy favored immigration status in all circumstances. Posthumous citizenship is authorized for noncitizen members of the armed forces who die during hostilities, but not for their spouses. When the government revokes the citizenship of someone because it was obtained through misconduct, and that person's spouse derived his or her citizenship from the marriage, the spouse's citizenship will also be revoked.

Some provisions of immigration law are designed to prevent misuse of marital status. The law calls for termination of the permanent resident status of an alien granted on the basis of marriage, if it is determined that the marriage was for the purpose of procuring the alien's entry to the United States, or if the marriage is annulled or terminated (other than through the death of a spouse) within two years.

The Congress recently limited the eligibility of qualified aliens for certain federal programs—such as SSI, Temporary Assistance for Needy Families (which will replace AFDC), and Social Services block grants—but it made a few exceptions, one of which directly benefits spouses of veterans. Aliens who are serving on active duty in the Armed Forces or who are honorably discharged veterans, and their spouses, remain eligible for these benefits in the same manner as a citizen. Federal law also provides that the incomes of the sponsor of an immigrant, and of the sponsor's spouse, are to be taken into account in determining the immigrant's eligibility for means-tested public benefits.

Category 7—Indians

The indigenous peoples of the United States have long had a special legal relationship with the federal government through treaties and laws that are classified to Title 25, Indians. Various laws set out the rights to tribal property of white men marrying Indian women, or of Indian women marrying white men, the evidence that is required, and the rights of children born of marriages between white men and Indian women.[8]

The law also establishes Indians' rights to develop descent and distribution rights regarding their property as long as they include certain provisions. Most relevant to this discussion is the right of a surviving spouse who is neither an Indian nor a member of the deceased spouse's tribe to elect a life estate in property that he or she is occupying at the time of the death of the other spouse. Another law governing rights of Navajo and Hopi Indians gives relocation benefits to spouses who relinquish their life estates.

Health services can also be made available to otherwise ineligible spouses of an eligible Indian if all such spouses are made eligible by an appropriate resolution of the governing body of the tribe. Health professionals seeking positions in the Indian Health Service and their spouses may be reimbursed for actual and reasonable expenses incurred in traveling to and from their homes to an area in which they could be assigned to allow them to evaluate the area with respect to the assignment.

Category 8—Trade, Commerce, and Intellectual Property

This category includes provisions concerning foreign or domestic business and commerce, from the following titles of the United States Code: Bankruptcy, Title 11; Banks and Banking, Title 12; Commerce and Trade, Title 15; Copyrights, Title 17; and Customs Duties, Title 19.

Federal law prescribes the right of debtors to seek bankruptcy protection and the rights of creditors when their debtors adopt that strategy. It expressly permits spouses to file jointly for bankruptcy protection. This may benefit both the debtors and their creditors: the married couple pays only one filing fee and creditors file only one claim.

Bankruptcy law prescribes how to distribute the assets of a bankrupt person, assigns specific priorities to different classes of creditors, and permits a bankrupt debtor to be "discharged" (i.e., released) from the obligation to repay certain debts. A former spouse of the debtor making a claim in a bankruptcy proceeding for payments pursuant to a divorce decree or separation agreement is given a higher priority than some other creditors. Also, a discharge in bankruptcy generally does not relieve a debtor of the obligation to pay alimony or support to a spouse or former spouse in

---

[8] The laws in this category dealing with marriage that use the terms "Indian" and "white" are more than 100 years old, and have not been amended since their enactment in 1888.

connection with a divorce decree or separation agreement.

The National Housing Act addresses the rights of mortgage borrowers. Banks often use a so-called due-on-sale clause in mortgage agreements that permits them to declare the loan payable in full if the borrower sells the property without their consent. The Act prohibits use of the due-on-sale clause in case of transfers of residential property from one spouse to another.

For some purposes, the laws regulating investment companies and advisers apply not only to the advisers themselves, but also to what the law terms "interested persons." "Interested persons" is defined to include the spouses of certain persons, of their parents, and of their children.

The Consumer Credit Protection Act regulates some aspects of garnishment of wages, a legal process whereby a creditor collects a debt by having the debtor's employer pay part of the debtor's wages directly to the creditor. The Act establishes that at most 25 percent of the disposable earnings of an individual can be withheld through garnishment. However, if the purpose of the garnishment is to enforce an order for the support of a spouse, the maximum is 60 percent or, if the wage earner is supporting a spouse (not the former spouse for whose benefit the support order was issued), 50 percent.

The Copyright Act gives renewal rights and termination rights, in some circumstances, to the widow or widower of the creator of a copyrighted work. The law defines "widow or widower" as the creator's surviving spouse under the law of the creator's domicile at the time of his or her death, whether or not the spouse subsequently remarries.

The amount of customs duty on imported merchandise depends on its value. Under the law, the actual transaction value—that is, how much the buyer paid the seller—may be used to establish value if the buyer and seller are not "related." For this purpose, spouses are deemed to be related. Also, certain countries that deny or restrict the ability of their citizens to emigrate in order to join "close relatives" in the United States can be penalized by the imposition of restrictions on their trade with the United States. "Close relative," for purposes of this law, includes a spouse.

Under the Fresh Cut Flowers and Fresh Cut Greens Promotion and Information Act of 1993, the federal government provides a mechanism for financing programs to strengthen the market for cut flowers and greens, through an assessment of "handlers" of these products whose annual sales exceed $750,000. Marital status comes into play in determining whether a handler meets the $750,000 threshold: for this purpose, sales by one spouse are attributed to the other.

Category 9—Financial Disclosure and Conflict of Interest

Federal law imposes obligations on Members of Congress, employees or officers of the federal government, and members of the boards of directors of some government-related or government-chartered entities, to prevent actual or apparent conflicts of interest. These individuals are required to disclose publicly certain gifts, interests, and transactions. Many of these requirements, which are found in 16 different titles of the United States Code, apply also to the individual's spouse.

The law regulates the conditions under which gifts from foreign governments and international organizations may be accepted by spouses of employees of the Postal Service, the Postal Rate Commission, certain government contractors, employees of the District of Columbia government, members of the uniformed services, Members of Congress, the President, and the Vice President. Employees of executive, legislative, and judicial agencies may not appoint relatives, including spouses, to agencies in which they serve or exercise control. The spouses of members of the Senate may not accept, in any calendar year, gifts worth more than $250, without getting a waiver.

Elsewhere in the Code are rules intended to prevent conflicts of interest on the part of members of various councils and boards. For instance, members of the boards of directors of the National Sheep Industry Improvement Center and the Alternative Agricultural Research and Commercialization Corporation are prohibited from participating in any matter pending before either board in which a spouse holds an interest. The law governing the members of Regional Fishery Management Councils is somewhat different. Members are required to disclose and make available for public inspection any financial interests they or their spouses might have in an activity that the councils might undertake.

Another variation in the treatment of conflict of interest involving spouses appears in connection with the National Foundation for Biomedical Research. Instead of prescribing conflict of interest rules for the Foundation, the Congress directed it to devise its own standards. However, those standards must ensure that officers, employees and agents of the Foundation (including members of the Board), and their spouses, avoid encumbrances that could result in a financial conflict of interest or a divided allegiance.

Category 10—Crimes and Family Violence

This category includes laws that implicate marriage in connection with criminal justice or family violence. The nature of these provisions varies greatly. Some deal with spouses as victims of crimes, others with spouses as perpetrators. These laws are found primarily in Title 18, Crimes and Criminal Procedure, but some, dealing with crime prevention and family violence, are in Title 42, The Public Health and Welfare.

Attempting to influence a United States official through threats directed at a spouse is a federal crime, as are killing, or attempting to kill, foreign officials or their spouses, or threatening to kill certain persons protected by the Secret Service, such as major presidential candidates and their spouses.

Under federal criminal statutes, spouses and others have some protections against domestic violence. It is a federal crime for a person to travel across a state line with the intent to injure a spouse or "intimate partner" if that person intentionally commits a crime of violence and causes bodily injury to the spouse or intimate partner. The term "spouse or intimate partner" is broadly defined to include a former spouse, someone who "shares a child in common" with the abuser, and someone who "cohabits or has cohabited with the abuser as a spouse."

In some cases, marriage can be a factor in triggering criminal liability. For example, a widow's or widower's entitlement to federal employee survivor payments ceases upon remarriage; such a widow or widower who remarries and continues to accept payment may, if found guilty, be fined or imprisoned.

Claiming marital status that does not exist can also be a crime. Falsely representing oneself to be the spouse or surviving spouse of an individual in order to elicit information about the Social Security number, date of birth, employment, wages, or benefits of that individual, is a felony.

Comprehensive crime control legislation directed the Attorney General to study the means by which abusive spouses obtain information concerning the addresses or locations of estranged or former spouses, despite the desire of the victims to have the information withheld. Congress also has charged the National Commission on Crime Prevention and Control to evaluate the adequacy of federal and state laws on sexual assault and the need for a more uniform statutory response to sex offenses. This mandate specifically addresses sexual assaults and other sex offenses committed by offenders who are known, or related by blood or marriage, to the victim.

Criminal justice grants are given to encourage arrest of domestic violence offenders; "domestic violence" includes an act of violence by a current or former spouse. Another provision gives nationals of the United States who are victims of acts of terrorism committed outside the United States, and their survivors, including spouses, a statutory right to bring a civil action for treble damages.

Category 11—Loans, Guarantees, and Payments in Agriculture

Under many federal loan programs, a spouse's income, business interests, or assets are taken into account for purposes of determining a person's eligibility to participate in the program. In other instances, marital status is a factor in determining the amount of federal assistance to which a person is entitled, or the repayment schedule.

Education loan programs are found primarily in Title 20, Education; housing loan programs for veterans are found in Title 38, Veterans' Benefits. Title 7, Agriculture, includes provisions governing agricultural price supports and loan programs that are affected by the spousal relationship.

Under the federal family education loan program, the income and assets of an independent student's spouse are attributed to the student for purposes of determining whether the student is eligible for a loan and, if so, the amount. Married couples may consolidate their separate student loans into one if they agree to be jointly and severally liable for repayment of the consolidated loan, without regard either to the amounts of the respective loan obligations to be consolidated or to any subsequent change in their marital status. Under the federal direct student loan program, the Secretary of Education, in order to determine the annual repayment amount when repayment is contingent on the borrower's income, may obtain information regarding the income not only of the borrower but also of the borrower's spouse. Repayment schedules are generally based on the adjusted gross income of both spouses.

Many of the laws governing veterans' benefits implicate marital status. Eligibility for assistance in borrowing for housing extends to the surviving spouses of veterans who die from a service-connected disability, and to the spouses of certain veterans who, for more than 90 days, have been missing in action, captured by hostile forces, or forcibly detained by a foreign government.

The laws governing agriculture include provisions for price supports and loan programs that are affected by marital status. For example, the law limits the amount of certain crop support payments that any one person can receive. For this purpose, a husband and wife are considered to be one person, except to the extent each may have owned property individually before the marriage. Also, agricultural loans for real estate, operating expenses, and emergencies may be made to "family farms," defined as those farms in which a majority interest is held by individuals related by marriage or blood.

Category 12—Federal Natural Resources and Related Laws

Federal law gives special rights to spouses in connection with a variety of transactions involving federal lands and other federal property. These transactions include purchase and sale of land by the federal government and lease by the government of water and mineral rights.

When the government purchases land for national battlefields, monuments, seashores, or parks, the law commonly allows those from whom the land is purchased and their spouses to continue to use and occupy it during their lifetimes. For example, those owning houses (and their spouses) when the Stones River National Battlefield and Sleeping Bear Dunes National Lakeshore were created have life estates in the land. Although these laws affect relatively few individuals, we found more than 40 such provisions in Title 16, Conservation.

In addition to playing a role under these provisions for the government to buy land, spousal relationship has also been a factor in determining priorities among potential buyers when the government is selling federal lands. For example, when Congress decided in 1955 to terminate ownership of land used by the Atomic Energy Commission and sell it to local entities and private parties, it generally barred any transfer of priorities for purchase, but allowed a husband and wife to exercise a priority in their joint names.

The marital relationship may affect whether an individual can be considered a surface mine owner with whom the Secretary of Labor can negotiate a lease. To be designated a surface mine owner, an individual must hold legal or equitable title to the land for a 3-year period and his or her principal residence must be on the land. In computing the 3-year period, the Secretary may include periods during which a relative by blood or marriage, including a spouse, owned the land.

Under laws governing reclamation and irrigation of lands by the federal government, the basic unit of ownership is 160 irrigable acres. Under certain conditions, if the death of a spouse causes lands in private ownership to become excess lands (having more than 160 acres) but those lands were eligible to receive water from a project under the Federal reclamation laws without a recordable contract, the Secretary of the Interior is authorized to furnish water to them, without requiring the contract, as long as the lands are owned by the surviving spouse. If the surviving spouse remarries, the exception no longer applies, and lands in excess of 160 irrigable acres are appraised in the usual manner.

Category 13—Miscellaneous

This category comprises laws that do not fit readily in any of the other categories and that in our judgment did not warrant a separate category. It is a heterogeneous mix of provisions from 14 titles of the United States Code.

Fourteen statutes in the Code that prohibit discrimination on the basis of marital status are listed in this category. For example, such discrimination is prohibited in executive agencies, and is unlawful for a creditor in private financial transactions.

This category includes the laws chartering various patriotic societies, such as the Veterans of Foreign Wars, that have as one of their purposes to assist the widows and children of servicemen or others. The Gold Star Wives of America and Navy Wives Clubs of America have one of our search terms in their titles.

We also included in this category laws related to the federal financing of presidential election campaigns. To be eligible for federal funds, candidates may not spend more than $50,000 of their own money or that of members of their immediate families for their campaigns. A spouse or a close relative's spouse is deemed to be a member of the candidate's immediate family for this purpose.

Chapter 4

SAME-SEX MARRIAGES*

Allison M. Smith

Currently neither federal law nor any state law affirmatively allows gay or lesbian couples to marry. On the federal level, Congress enacted the Defense of Marriage Act (DOMA) to prohibit recognition of same-sex marriages for purposes of federal enactments. States, such as Alaska, Hawaii, Nebraska and Nevada have enacted state constitutional amendments limiting marriage to one man and one woman. Thirty-six other states have enacted statutes limiting marriage in some manner.[1] A chart summarizing these various approaches is included at the end of this report.

DEFENSE OF MARRIAGE ACT (DOMA)[2]

In 1996, Congress enacted the DOMA "[t]o define and protect the institution of marriage." It allows all states, territories, possessions, and Indian tribes to refuse to recognize an act of any other jurisdiction that

---

* Excerpted fro CRS Report RL31994. July 15, 2003.

[1] These states are: Alabama, Arizona, Arkansas, California, Colorado, Delaware, Florida, Georgia, Idaho, Illinois, Indiana, Iowa, Kansas, Kentucky, Louisiana, Maryland, Michigan, Minnesota, Mississippi, Missouri, Montana, Nevada, New Hampshire, North Carolina, North Dakota, Oklahoma, Pennsylvania, South Carolina, South Dakota, Tennessee, Texas, Utah, Virginia, Washington, West Virginia, and Wyoming.

[2] Pub. L. No. 104-199,110 Stat 2419 (codified at 1 U.S.C. § 7 and 28 U.S.C. § 1738C).

designates a relationship between individuals of the same sex as a marriage,
hi part, DOMA states:

> No State, territory, or possession of the United States, or Indian tribe, shall
> be required to give effect to any public act, record, or judicial proceeding of
> any other State, territory, possession, or tribe respecting a relationship
> between persons of the same sex that is treated as a marriage under the laws
> of such other State, territory, possession, or tribe, or a right or claim arising
> from such relationship.[3]

Furthermore, DOMA goes on to declare that the terms "marriage" and
"spouse," as used in federal enactments, exclude homosexual marriage.

> In determining the meaning of any Act of Congress, or of any ruling,
> regulation, or interpretation of the various administrative bureaus and
> agencies of the United States, the word 'marriage' means only a legal union
> between one man and one woman as husband and wife, and the word
> 'spouse' refers only to a person of the opposite sex who is a husband or a
> wife.[4]

POTENTIAL CONSTITUTIONAL CHALLENGES TO DOMA[5]

Full Faith and Credit Clause

Some argue that DOMA is an unconstitutional exercise of Congress'
authority under the full faith and credit clause of the U.S. Constitution.[6]

---

[3] 28U.S.C. §1738C.

[4] 1 U.S.C. § 7.

[5] It should be noted that a court has yet to determine the constitutionality of the DOMA. In a
federal tax-evasion case, the defendant claimed that he and his domestic partner were
"economic partners" who should be afforded filing status equivalent to that of a married
couple, and argued that DOMA was unconstitutional. The Seventh Circuit refused to onsider
the claim, holding that DOMA "was not in effect during the 10-year period for
which Mueller was assessed deficiencies and, thus, is not at issue here." *Mueller* v.
Commissioner, 2001 WL 522388, at 1 (7th Cir. Apr. 6, 2001). Mueller later raised the same
challenge in a dispute over a tax return when DOMA was in effect, but the Seventh Circuit
held that the law did not apply because "Mr. Mueller did not try to have his same-sex
relationship recognized as a marriage under Illinois law..." *Mueller v. Commissioner*, No.
4743-00,2002 WL 1401297, at *1 (7th Cir. June 26, 2002).

[6] U.S. Const, art. IV, § 1.

Article IV, section 1 of the Constitution, the Full Faith and Credit Clause states:

> Full Faith and Credit shall be given in each State to the public Acts, Records, and judicial Proceedings of every other State; And the Congress may by general Laws prescribe the Manner in which such Acts, Records and Proceedings shall be proved, and the Effect thereof.

Opponents argue that, while Congress has authority to pass laws that enable acts, judgments and the like to be given effect in other States, it has no constitutional power to pass a law permitting States to deny full faith and credit to another State's laws and judgments.[7] Conversely, some argue that DOMA does nothing more than simply restate the power granted to the States by the full faith and credit clause.[8] While there is no judicial precedent on this issue, it would appear that Congress' general authority to "prescribe...the effect" of public acts arguably gives it discretion to define the "effect" so mat a particular public act is not due full faith and credit. It would appear that the plain reading of the clause would encompass both expansion and contraction.

Equal Protection

Congress' authority to legislate in this manner under the full faith and credit clause, if the analysis set out above is accepted, does not conclude the matter. There are constitutional constraints upon federal legislation. One that is relevant is the equal protection clause and the effect of the Supreme Court's decision in *Romer* v. *Evans,*[9] which struck down under the equal protection clause a referendum-adopted provision of the Colorado Constitution, which repealed local ordinances that provided civil-rights protections for gay persons and which prohibited all governmental action designed to protect homosexuals from discrimination. The Court held that, under the equal protection clause, legislation adverse to homosexuals was to

---

[7] See 142 Cong. Rec. S5931-33 (June 6,1996) (statement introducing Professor Laurence H. Tribe's letter into the record concluding that DOMA "would be an unconstitutional attempt by Congress to limit the full faith and credit clause of the Constitution.").

[8] See Paige E. Chabora, Congress' Power Under the Full Faith and Credit Clause and the Defense of Marriage Act of 1996, 76 Neb. L. Rev. 604, 621-35 (1997).

[9] 517 U.S. 620 (1996).

be scrutinized under a "rational basis" standard of review.[10] The classification failed to pass even mis-deferential standard of review, because it imposed a special disability on homosexuals not visited on any other class of people and it could not be justified by any of the arguments made by the State. The State argued that its purpose for the amendment was two-fold: (1) to respect the freedom of association rights of other citizens, such as landlords and employers) who objected to homosexuality; and (2) to serve the state's interest in conserving resources to fight discrimination against other protected groups.

DOMA can be distinguished from the Colorado amendment. DOMA's legislative history indicates that it was intended to protect federalism interests and state sovereignty in the area of domestic relations, historically a subject of almost exclusive state concern. Moreover, it permits but does not require States to deny recognition to same-sex marriages in other States, affording States with strong public policy concerns the discretion to effectuate that policy. Thus, it can be argued that DOMA is grounded not in hostility to homosexuals but in an intent to afford the States the discretion to act as their public policy on same-sex marriage dictates.

Substantive Due Process (Right to Privacy)

Another possibly applicable constitutional constraint is the Due Process Clause of the Fourteenth Amendment and the effect of me Supreme Court's decision in *Lawrence* v. *Texas*[11] which struck down under the due process clause a state statute criminalizing certain private sexual acts between homosexuals. The Court held that the Fourteenth Amendment's due process privacy guarantee extends to protect consensual sex between adult homosexuals. The Court noted that the Due Process right to privacy protects certain personal decisions from governmental interference. These personal decisions include issues regarding contraceptives, abortion, marriage, procreation, and family relations.[12] The Court extended this right to privacy to cover adult consensual homosexual sodomy.

---

[10] *Id.*
[11] No. 02-102,2003 U.S. LEXIS 5013 (June 26, 2003). For a legal analysis of this decision, refer to CRS Report RL31681, *Homosexuality and the Constitution: A Legal Analysis of the Supreme Court Ruling in Lawrence* v. *Texas* by Jody Feder.
[12] *Lawrence* v. *Texas,* No. 02-102, 2003 U.S. LEXIS 5013, at *28 (June 26,2003).

It is currently unclear what impact, if any, the Court's decision in *Lawrence* will have on legal challenges to laws prohibiting same-sex marriage. On the one hand, this decision can be viewed as affirming a broad constitutional right to sexual privacy. Conversely, the Court distinguished this case from cases involving minors and "whether the government must give formal recognition to any relationship that homosexual persons seek to enter."[13] Courts may seek to distinguish statutes prohibiting same-sex marriage from statutes criminalizing homosexual conduct. Courts may view the preservation of the institution of marriage as sufficient justification for statutes banning same-sex marriage. Moreover, courts may view the public recognition of marriage differently than the sexual conduct of homosexuals in the privacy of their own homes.

INTERSTATE RECOGNITION OF MARRIAGE

DOMA opponents assume that the Full Faith and Credit Clause would obligate States to recognize same-sex marriages contracted in States in which they are authorized. This conclusion is far from evident as this clause applies principally to the interstate recognition and enforcement of judgments.[14] It is settled law that final judgments are entitled to full faith and credit, regardless of other states' public policies, provided the issuing state had jurisdiction over the parties and the subject matter.[15] The Full Faith and Credit Clause has rarely been used by courts to validate marriages because marriages are not "legal judgments."

As such, questions concerning the validity of an out-of-state marriage are generally resolved without reference to the Full Faith and Credit Clause. In the legal sense, marriage is a "civil contract" created by the States which establishes certain duties and confers certain benefits.[16] Validly entering the contract creates the marital status; the duties and benefits attached by a State

---

[13] *Id.* at *36.

[14] See H.R. Rep. 104-664,1996 U.S.C.C.A.N. 2905 (stating that "marriage licensure is not a judgment"). See also, 28 U.S.C. § 1738 (defining which acts, records and judicial proceeding are afforded fall faith and credit).

[15] *Restatement (Second) of Conflict of Laws* § 107.

[16] On the state level, common examples of nonnegotiable marital rights and obligations include: distinct income tax filing status; public assistance such as health and welfare benefits; default rules concerning community property distribution and control; dower, curtesy and inheritance rights; child custody, child agreements; name change rights; spouse and marital communications privileges in legal proceedings; and the right to bring wrongful death, and certain other, legal actions.

are incidents of that status. As such, the general tendency, based on comity rather than on compulsion under the Full Faith and Credit Clause, is to recognize marriages contracted in other States even if they could not have been celebrated in the recognizing State.

The general rule of validation for marriage is to look to the law of the place where the marriage was celebrated. A marriage satisfying the contracting State's requirements will usually be held valid everywhere.[17] Many States provide by statute that a marriage that is valid where contracted is valid within the State. This "place of celebration" rule is then subject to a number of exceptions, most of which are narrowly construed. The most common exception to the "place of celebration" rule is for marriages deemed contrary to the forum's strong public policy. Several States, such as Connecticut,[18] Idaho,[19] Illinois,[20] Kansas,[21] Missouri,[22] Pennsylvania,[23] South Carolina,[24] Tennessee[25] and West Virginia,[26] provide an exception to this general rule by declaring out-of-state marriages void if against the State's public policy or if entered into with the intent to evade the law of the State. This exception applies only where another State's law violates "some fundamental principle of justice, some prevalent conception of good morals, some deep-rooted tradition of the common weal."[27]

Section 283 of the Restatement (Second) of Law provides:

> (1) The validity of marriage will be determined by the local law of the state which, with respect to the particular issue, has the most significant relationship to the spouses and the marriage under the principles stated in § 6.

---

[17] See 2 Restatement (Second) of Conflict of Laws § 283.
[18] Conn. Gen Stat. Ann. § 45a-803-4.
[19] Idaho Code §32-209.
[20] 750 Hl. Comp. Stat. 5/201.
[21] Kan. Stat Ann. §23-101.
[22] Mo. Rev. Stat §451.022.
[23] Pa. Stat Ann. tit 23 § 1704.
[24] S.C. Code Ann. §20-1-10.
[25] Tenn. Code Ann. § 36-3-113.
[26] W.Va. Code §48-2-603.
[27] *Loucks v. Standard Oil Co.,* 120 N.E. 198, 202 (N.Y. 1918)(defining public policy as a valid reason for closing the forum to suit); see e.g. *Langan* v. *St. Vincent Hosp.,* 2003 N.Y. Misc. LEXIS 673 (stating that New York adheres to the general rule that "marriage contracts, valid where made, are valid everywhere, unless contrary to natural laws or statutes"); *Shea* v. *Shea,* 63 N.E.2d 113 (N.Y. 1945)(finding that a common law marriage validly contracted in another state should not be recognized as common law marriage in New York as it was prohibited by statute).

(2) A marriage which satisfies the requirements of the state where the marriage was contracted will everywhere be recognized as valid unless it violates the strong public policy of another state which had the most significant relationship to the spouses and the marriage at the time of the marriage.

PENDING STATE LITIGATION

Massachusetts, unlike approximately thirty-seven States and the federal government, has not adopted a "defense of marriage statute" defining marriage as a union between a man and woman.[28] On April 11, 2001, a Boston-based, homosexual rights group, Gay Lesbian Advocates and Defenders filed suit against the Massachusetts Department of Public Health on behalf of seven same-sex couples. The plaintiffs claimed that "refusing same-sex couples the opportunity to apply for a marriage license" violates Massachusetts' law and various portions of the Massachusetts Constitution. GLAD's brief attempts to find a fundamental right to marry "the person of one's choosing" in the due process provisions of the Massachusetts Constitution and asserts that the marriage laws, which allow both men and women to marry, violate equal protection provisions.[29]

The Superior Court rejected the plaintiffs' arguments after exploring the application of the word marriage, the construction of marriage statutes and finally, the historical purpose of marriage. The trial court found that based on history and the actions of the people's elected representatives, a right to same-sex marriage was not so rooted in tradition that a failure to recognize it violated fundamental liberty, nor was it implicit in ordered liberty.[30] Moreover, the court held that in excluding same-sex couples from marriage, the Commonwealth did not deprive them of substantive due process, liberty, or freedom of speech or association.[31] The court went on to find that limiting marriage to opposite-sex couples was rationally related to a legitimate state interest of encouraging procreation.[32]

---

[28] It should be noted that hi *Adoption of Tammy*, 619 N.E. 2d 315 (Mass. 1993), the Supreme Judicial Court has interpreted "marriage" to mean "the union of one man and one woman."

[29] *Hilary Goodridge* v. *Dept. of Public Health*, No. 01-1647-A, 2002 Mass. Super LEXIS 153 (Suffolk County, Super. Ct May 7, 2002).

[30] *Id.*

[31] *Id.*

[32] *Id.*

The case has been appealed to the Supreme Judicial Court of Massachusetts. A decision is expected soon.

PENDING FEDERAL LEGISLATION

On May 21, 2003, HJ.Res. 56, a proposed constitutional amendment was introduced. The text of the amendment is as follows:

> Marriage in the United States shall consist only of the union of a man and a woman. Neither this Constitution or the constitution of any State, nor state or federal law, shall be construed to require that marital status or the legal incidents thereof be conferred upon unmarried couples or groups.

While uniformity may be achieved upon ratification of such an amendment, States would no longer have the flexibility of defining marriage within their borders. Moreover, States maybe prohibited from recognizing a same-sex marriage performed and recognized outside of the United States.[33] It appears that this amendment would not impact a State's ability to define civil unions or domestic partnerships and the benefits conferred upon such.

However, an issue may arise regarding the time in which an individual is considered a man or a woman. As the first official document to indicate a person's sex, the designation on the birth certificate "usually controls the sex designation on all later documents."[34] Some courts have held that sexual identity for purposes of marriage is determined by the sex stated on the birth certificate, regardless of subsequent sexual reassignment.[35] However, some argue that this method is flawed, as an infant's sex may be misidentified at birth and the individual may subsequently identify with and conform his or her biology to another sex upon adulthood.[36]

---

[33] It appears that the Netherlands, Belgium and Ontario, Canada are the only international jurisdictions that sanction and/or recognize a same-sex union as a "marriage," per se.

[34] Julie A. Greenberg, Defining Male and Female: Intersexuality and the Collision Between Law and Biology, 41 Ariz. L. Rev. 265,309 (1999) (discussing biological characteristics and sexual identity).

[35] See e.g., *In re Estate of Gardiner*, 42 P.3d 120 (Kan. 2002); *Uttleton* v. *Prange*, 9 S.W. 3d 223 (Tex. App. 1999); but see, *M.T.* v. *J.T.*, 355 A.2d 204 (N.J. 1976)(determining an individual's sexual classification for the purpose of marriage encompasses a mental component as well as an anatomical component).

[36] If a mistake was made on the original birth certificate, an amended certificate will sometimes be issued if accompanied by an affidavit from a physician or a court order.

CONCLUSION

States currently possess the authority to decide whether to recognize an out-of-state marriage. The Full Faith and Credit Clause has rarely been used by States to validate marriages because marriages are not "legal judgments." With respect to cases decided under the Full Faith and Credit Clause that involve conflicting State statutes, the Supreme Court generally examines the significant aggregation of contacts the forum has with the parties and the occurrence or transaction to decide which State's law to apply. Similarly, based upon generally accepted legal principles, States routinely decide whether a marriage validly contracted in another jurisdiction will be recognized in-State by examining whether it has a significant relationship with the spouses and the marriage.

Congress is empowered under the Full Faith and Credit Clause of the Constitution to prescribe the manner that public acts, commonly understood to mean legislative acts, records, and proceedings shall be proved and the effect of such acts, records, and proceedings in other States.[37]

The Supreme Court's decisions hi *Romer* v. *Colorado* and *Lawrence v. Texas* may present different issues concerning DOMA's constitutionality. Basically *Romer* appears to stand for the proposition that legislation targeting gays and lesbians is constitutionally impermissible under the Equal Protection Clause unless the legislative classification bears a rational relationship to a legitimate State purpose. Because same-sex marriages are singled out for differential treatment, DOMA appears to create a legislative classification for equal protection purposes that must meet a rational basis test. It is possible that DOMA could survive constitutional scrutiny under *Romer* inasmuch as the statute was enacted to protect die traditional institution of marriage. Moreover, DOMA does not prohibit States from recognizing same-sex marriage if they so choose.

Lawrence appears to stand for the proposition that the zone of privacy protected by the Due Process Clause of the Fourteen Amendment extends to adult, consensual sex between homosexuals. Lawrence's implication for

---

[37] It should be noted that only on five occasions previous to the DOMA has Congress enacted legislation based upon this power. The first, passed in 1790 (1 Stat. 122, codified at 28 U.S.C. § 1738), provides for ways to authenticate acts, records and judicial proceedings. The second, dating from 1804 (2 Stat. 298, codified at 28 U.S.C. 1738), provides methods of authenticating non-judicial records. Three other Congressional enactments pertain to modifiable family law orders (child custody, 28 U.S.C. § 1738A, child support (28 U.S.C. § 1738B) and domestic protection (18 U.S.C. § 2265)).

statutes banning same-sex marriages and the constitutional validity of the DOMA are unclear.

Table 1. State Statutes Defining "Marriage"

State	Statute	Marriage Definition[a]	Non-Recognition
Alabama	ALA. CODE § 30-1-19 (2003)	X	X
Alaska	ALASKA STAT. § 25.05.01 1 (2003)	X	
Arizona	ARIZ. REV. STAT. § 25-101 (2003)		X
Arkansas	ARK. CODE ANN. § 9-11-109 (2003)	X	
California	CAL. FAM. CODE § 300 (2003)	X	
Colorado	COLO. REV. STAT. § 14-2-104 (2003)	X	
Connecticut*	Judicial Interpretation		X[b]
Delaware	DEL. CODE ANN. tit. 13 § 101 (2002)		X
Florida	FLA. STAT. Ch. 741.04 (2002)	X	
Georgia	GA. CODE ANN. § 19-3-3.1 (2002)		X
Hawaii	HAW. REV. STAT. ANN. § 572-1 (2003)	X	
Idaho*	IDAHO CODE § 32-209 (2003)	X	
Illinois*	750 ILL. COMP. STAT. 5/201 (2003)	X	X
Indiana	IND. CODE ANN. § 31-11-1-1 (2003)	X	X
Iowa	IOWA CODE § 595.2 (2003)	X	
Kansas*	KAN.. STAT. ANN. § 23-101 (2002)	X	
Kentucky	KY. REV. STAT. ANN. § 402.020 (2002)		X
Louisiana	LA. Civ. CODE art. 86 (2003)	X	
Maine	ME. REV. STAT. ANN. tit. 19, § 701 (2003)		X
Maryland	MD. CODE ANN. FAM. LAW § 2-201 (2002)	X	
Massachusetts	Judicial Interpretation	X[c]	
Michigan	MICH. COMP. LAWS § 551.1 (2003)	X	X
Minnesota	MINN. STAT. § 517.01 (2002)	X	
Mississippi	Miss. CODE ANN. § 93-1-1 (2003)		X
Missouri*	MO. REV. STAT. §451.022 (2003)		X
Montana	MONT. CODE ANN. § 40-1-103 (2002)	X	
Nebraska	NEB. REV. STAT. ANN. art. 1, § 29 (2002)		X
Nevada	NEV. REV. STAT. ANN. §122.020 (2003)	X	
New Hampshire	N.H. REV. STAT. ANN. § 457:2 (2002)		X
New Jersey	Judicial Interpretation	x[d]	
New Mexico	N.M. STAT. ANN § 40-1-1 (2002)	X[e]	
New York	Judicial Interpretation	x[f]	
North Carolina	N.C. GEN. STAT. § 51-1.2 (2003)		X
North Dakota	N.D. CENT. CODE § 14-03-01 (2002)	X	
Ohio	OHIO REV. CODE ANN. §3 101 (2002)	X[g]	
Oklahoma	OKLA. STAT. tit. 43 § 3.1 (2003)		X
Oregon	OR. REV. STAT. § 106.010 (2001)	X	
Pennsylvania*	PA. STAT. ANN. tit. 23 § 1704 (2002)		X
Rhode Island	R.I. GEN. LAWS § 15-1-1 (2002)	X[h]	

State	Statute	Marriage Definition[a]	Non-Recognition
South Carolina*	S.C. CODE ANN. § 20-1-10 (2002)		X
South Dakota	S. D. CODIFIED LAWS § 25-1-1 (2002)	X	
Tennessee*	TENN. CODE. ANN. § 36-3-113 (2003)	X	
Texas	TEX. FAM. CODE ANN. § 2.001 (2002)	X	
Utah	UTAH CODE ANN. § 30-1-2 (2003)		X
Vermont	VT. STAT. ANN. tit. 15 § 8 (2003)	X	
Virginia	VA. CODE ANN. § 20-45.2 (2003)		X
Washington	WASH. REV. CODE ANN. § 26.04.010 (2003)	X	
West Virginia*	W. VA. CODE § 48-2-603 (2003)		X
Wisconsin	Wis. STAT. § 765.01 (2002)	X[1]	
Wyoming	WYO. STAT. § 20-1-101 (2003)	X	
Puerto Rico	P.R. LAWS ANN. tit. 3 1, § 221 (2002)	X	

* denotes statute establishing same-sex union as violation of state's public policy

a. Marriage consists of a contract between one man and one woman.

b. Since nothing in the statute, legislative history, court rules, case law, or public policy permitted same-sex marriage or recognized the parties* Vermont civil union as a marriage, the trial court lacked jurisdiction to dissolve the union.

c. The Supreme Judicial Court has interpreted "marriage," within Massachusetts' statutes, "as the union of one man and one *woman.*" *Adoption of Tammy,* 619 N.E.2d 315 (1993).

d. Although no specific language in this statute or other New Jersey marriage statutes prohibits same-sex marriages, the meaning of marriage as a heterosexual institution was so firmly established that the court could not disregard its plain meaning and the clear intent of the legislature. *Rutgers Council* v. *Rutgers State University,* 689 A.2d 828 (1997).

e. Marriage is a civil contract requiring consent of parties

f. Marriage has been traditionally defined as the voluntary union of one man and one woman as husband and wife. See e.g. *Fisher v. Fisher,* 250 N.Y. 313,165 N. E. 460 (1929). A basic assumption, therefore, is that one of the two parties to the union must be male and the other must be female. On the basis of this assumption, the New York courts have consistently viewed it essential to the formation of a marriage that the parties be of opposite sexes. However, in *Langan v. St. Vincent Hosp.,* 2003 N.Y. Misc. LEXIS 673, the court found that New York's statutes did not prohibit recognition of a same-sex union nor was such a union against New York's public policy on marriage. As such, the court recognized the same-sex partner as a spouse for purposes of New York's wrongful death statute.

g. Males age 18 and females age 16, not nearer of kin than second cousins, and not having a husband or wife living, may be joined in marriage.

h. Men are forbidden to marry kindred.

i. Marriage, so far as its validity at law is concerned, is a civil contract, to which the consent of the parties capable in law of contracting is essential, and which creates the legal status of husband and wife.

Chapter 5

SAME-SEX ADOPTIONS

Alison M. Smith

INTRODUCTION

State laws concerning the eligibility of homosexuals to adopt vary. Some states statutorily prohibit such action, while others are silent on the issue, leaving interpretation to the courts. This chapter summarizes state laws concerning non-relative adoption by homosexual individuals and couples.

Consistent with other areas of family law, adoption statutes are promulgated by state legislatures in accordance with public policy considerations that often include providing for the best interests of the child, achieving finality in the placement of children and promoting stability in family relations. Thus, individual states have different statutes regarding non-relative adoption by homosexual individuals and couples.[1]

Most states currently permit an individual gay or lesbian adult to adopt a minor child subject, as in any adoption, to a finding by a judge, that adoption by that individual is in the child's best interest.[2] No state currently sanctions

---

[*] Excerpted from CRS Report RS21191 April 9, 2002.

[1] The related issue of second parent adoption is beyond the scope of this report. A second parent adoption is a legal procedure which allows a same-sex co-parent to adopt his or her partner's child.

[2] Numerous factors converge and influence this standard, including the home environment, stability of the parents, the time a parent and child spend together, the quality of the relationship between parent and child, sexual conduct and criminal background of the parents, as well as other factors the court deems appropriate. See 2 Am. Jur. 2d Adoption §

in statute adoption by lesbian or homosexual couples. State statutes concerning the eligibility of homosexuals to adopt range from Florida's statutory prohibition[3] on homosexual individuals adopting to Mississippi's statute barring adoption by same-sex couples[4] to Utah's prohibition on unmarried couples, heterosexual or homosexual, from adopting.[5] Many state statutes are silent on the issue, leaving the subject open to interpretation by courts.[6] For example, the Ohio Supreme Court permitted the adoption of a "special needs" child by a homosexual, stating that there is a need to review adoption applications on a case-by-case basis without exacting any clear-cut rules regarding homosexual applicants.[7] Similarly, a New Jersey court allowed a homosexual couple to adopt a special needs child whom they fostered for approximately two years.[8]

A number of states have introduced legislation concerning the eligibility of homosexual individuals and couples to adopt. Legislation was introduced to ban homosexual adoptions in Alabama,[9] South Carolina,[10] Michigan,[11]

---

137. Florida is currently the only state which prohibits homosexual individuals from adopting. Fla. Stat. Ann. 63.042.

[3] Fla. Stat. Ann. 63.042.

[4] Miss Ann. Code § 93-17-3(2).

[5] See, e.g., Utah Stat § 78-30-1.

[6] See, e.g., *In re Lace,* 516 N.W.2d 678,686 (Wis. 1994) (barring adoption of mother's daughter by mother's female partner because statutory scheme "'balances society's interest in promoting stable, legally recognized families with its interests in promoting the best interests of die children involved.") see also, e.g., *Adoption of Tammy,* 619 N.E.2d 315 (Mass. 1993) (holding that Massachusetts law did not preclude same-sex cohabitants from jointly adopting a *child); Adoptions of B.L V.B & E.L. V.B.,* 628 A.2d 1271 (Vt. 1993) (holding Vermont law does not require the termination of a natural mother's parental rights if her children are adopted by a person to whom she is not married, if it is in the best interests of the children).

[7] *In re Adoption of Charles B.,* 552 N.E. 2d 884 (Ohio 1990). "Special needs" child refers to the fact that Charles B. suffered from leukemia, possible brain damage from fetal alcohol syndrome, a low I.Q., and a speech impediment. His natural family abused him and he lived in four different foster homes. These factors led the court to believe that Charles B. would be better off with his adoptive parent, a homosexual, instead of in an institution or moving from foster home to foster home. *Id.*

[8] See, Joyce F. Sims, *"Homosexuals Battling the Barriers of Mainstream Adoption-And Winning,"* 23 T. Marshall L. Rev. 551, 581 (1998). Subsequently, me parties entered into an agreement in which gay and unmarried couples will be measured by the same adoption standards as married couples. Furthermore, no couple could be barred from adoption based on their sexual orientation or marital status.

[9] H.R.J. Res. 35, Reg. Sess. (Ala. 1998).

[10] H.R. 3179,112th Sess. (S.C. 1997).

[11] See H.R. 6236, 89th Leg., Reg. Sess. (Mich. 1998)(stating that a "child shall not be placed with a prospective adoptive parent and the court shall not issue an adoption order if a person authorized to place the child or the court authorized to issue the order has reliable information that the prospective adoptive parent is homosexual.").

Arkansas,[12] Indiana,[13] Texas,[14] and Oklahoma.[15] However, none of these bills became law. In 1999, New Hampshire repealed its statute prohibiting adoption by homosexuals.[16]

In 2000, Mississippi and Utah also passed legislation affecting homosexuals' eligibility to adopt. Mississippi prohibits adoption by homosexual couples.[17] Utah's legislation bars all unmarried couples, heterosexual or same-sex, from state-sponsored adoptions.[18] The statute doesn't expressly prohibit adoption by single people, nor does it ban same-sex couples from adopting from private agencies.[19]

Recently, in *Lofton v. Kearney,*[20] a Florida district court held that a Florida statute denying homosexuals the right to adopt children does not violate the constitutional guarantees of equal protection or due process.[21] The plaintiffs alleged that, as applied to them, Florida's ban on gay adoption infringed on the rights to privacy, family integrity, and intimate association that are embedded in the First Amendment and the Due Process Clause of the Fourteenth Amendment.[22] Plaintiff's second claim asserted that the Florida statute violated the Equal Protection Clause of the Fourteenth Amendment.[23]

The court rejected both arguments. Addressing the due process argument, the court emphasized there is no fundamental right to adopt, nor a fundamental right to be adopted.[24] Thus, the court reasoned there can be no fundamental right to apply for adoption.[25] As such, the liberty interest biological parents enjoy in raising their children without state interference could not be extended to a foster parent or guardian based merely on the

---

[12] See H.R. 2232, 82nd Leg., Reg. Sess. (Ark. 1999).

[13] See H.R, 1055, 111th Leg., Reg. Sess. (Ind. 1999).

[14] See H.R. 382, 76th Leg., Reg. Sess. (Tex. 1999). The Texas bill mandated an "investigation to determine whether homosexual conduct is occurring or likely to occur in the adoptive home."

[15] See H.R. 1280, 47th Leg., 1st Sess. (Okla. 1999).

[16] N.H. Stat. § 170-B:4. In the wake of this enactment, a legislative service request was filed on September 22, 1999 providing for a reinstatement of the prohibition on adoption and foster parenting by homosexual persons. See Legis. Serv. Reg. 2012 (N.H. 1999).

[17] Miss Ann. Code § 93-17-3(2).

[18] See, e.g., Utah Stat. § 78-30-1.

[19] *Id.*

[20] 157 F.Supp.2d 1372 (S.D. Fla. 2001).

[21] *Id*

[22] *Id* at 1379.

[23] *Id.*

[24] *Id.*

[25] *Id.*

existence of strong emotional ties between the foster parent or guardian and the child.[26]

Addressing the equal protection argument, the court rejected the plaintiffs' assertion that the court should apply strict scrutiny hi analyzing the statute. Relying on *Romer v. Evans*[27] the district court reasoned that homosexuals do not constitute a suspect or quasi-suspect class for the purpose of equal protection analysis. As such, the court reasoned that "while homosexuals are protected by the Equal Protection Clause, government action classifying individuals on the basis of homosexuality or homosexual conduct must be analyzed under the rational basis test." Applying this analysis, the court found that it was rational to believe that a heterosexual, married couple would provide children with a more stable home life, "proper gender role modeling [,] and [minimal] social stigmatization" as compared to homosexual parents.[28]

The ACLU, representing the plaintiffs in this matter, filed an appeal to the U. S. Court of Appeals for the 11th Circuit in Atlanta.[29] This will mark the first time a federal appeals court will weigh the constitutionality of banning gay adoptions in the United States.

---

[26] *Id.*

[27] 517 U.S. 620 (1996)(invalidating an amendment to the Colorado state constitution prohibiting all governmental action designed to protect homosexuals from discrimination).

[28] *Lofton v. Kearney,* 157 F.Supp.2d at 1384.

[29] Landmark ACLU Case Challenging Florida's Gay Adoption Ban Reaches Federal Appeals Court (February 14, 2002). This press release can be obtained at [http://www.aclu. org/news/2002/n)21402a.html]

Chapter 6

PROTECTING MARRIAGE BY CONSTRAINING THE COURTS

John Hostettler

Over the last 50 years, our Federal judiciary has engaged in a quiet revolution. Rejecting a century and a half of American jurisprudence, the courts have worked toward establishing a new form of government where they are completely independent, free from checks and balances, and without accountability to what had once been a government of the people.

With growing boldness, judges are moving us away from a constitutional republic constructed on a three-tiered system of government that's ultimately accountable to its citizens. By increasing their sphere of influence and assuming duties limited to the legislative and executive branches, the courts have effectively established an oligarchy, a form of government where a handful of people wield the power.

Judges, Thomas Jefferson pointed out early in our history, "have the same passions for party, for power, for privilege of their corps," as anyone else. As students of history and political science, our Founders understood the corruptive influence of power and purposely erected a government with divided authority. Each branch had distinct, unambiguous roles reserved to it.

That fact has been forgotten by too many of today's scholars, journalists and judges. When the courts issue an unconstitutional opinion, when they assume constitutional powers reserved for the other branches of government, we are told that the Congress, the executive branch and ultimately the people are without recourse.

This is nonsense. The Founders never intended for the judiciary to be the most powerful branch. On the contrary, "the judiciary is beyond comparison the weakest of the three departments of power," Alexander Hamilton wrote in the Federalist Papers. He added that the constitutional powers granted to legislative and executive branches were checks against judicial "misconstructions."

This was obvious even to John Marshall, chief justice of the 1803 Supreme Court that decided the *Marbury v. Madison* case. This decision is often said to have established judicial supremacy over constitutional matters. But Marshall, in an 1804 letter to a fellow justice regarding impeachment, argued that "an appellate jurisdiction in the legislature" was the proper fix for "legal opinions deemed unsound" by that legislature. In other words, the supposed father of judicial supremacy believed *Congress* had a duty to correct unconstitutional judicial rulings.

I agree. I believe the time is ripe for dismantling the altar of judicial supremacy, restoring the courts' accountability and returning the government to the people.

With that in mind, I introduced legislation this week limiting the federal courts' ability to set a national precedent undermining the institution of marriage.

The Marriage Protection Act, as the bill is known, removes jurisdiction from certain federal courts over questions pertaining to the 1996 Defense of Marriage Act, better known as DOMA.

DOMA says that no state is required to give full faith and credit to a marriage license issued by another state if that relationship is between two people of the same sex. It also defines the terms "marriage" and "spouse" for purposes of federal law as terms only applying to relationships between people of the opposite sex.

DOMA is good law and passed with broad support, but many are concerned that an activist federal court will find some way to overturn it and create a "right" to homosexual marriage.

The Marriage Protection Act addresses that possibility by removing the Supreme Court's appellate jurisdiction, as well as inferior federal courts' original and appellate jurisdiction, over DOMA's full faith and credit provision. It also removes appellate jurisdiction from the Supreme Court and inferior federal courts over DOMA's marriage definition.

This is the sort of legislative check the Founders intended. Article I, Section 8 and Article III, Sections 1 and 2 of the Constitution grant Congress the authority to establish inferior federal courts, determine their jurisdiction and make exceptions to the Supreme Court's appellate jurisdiction. By implementing this legislative power we can preserve each state's traditional right to determine its own marriage policies without federal court interference. (For instance, a state of appeals court in Arizona last week upheld that state's DOMA law.)

Marriage is a divinely ordained institution, not a social experiment to be reinvented and redefined by a handful of unelected elites. The courts do not have the constitutional authority to redefine words and institutions in order to comport with judges' ideologies or whims.

But if recent history is a guide, that won't stop them. For too long the courts have felt free to exceed their constitutional boundaries. We've forgotten that our Constitution established a government of "We the People" - and the people, through their elected officials, have the final say in Constitutional questions.

THE MARRIAGE PROTECTION ACT

What it Does

- The Marriage Protection Act removes jurisdiction from certain federal courts over questions pertaining to the 1996 Defense of Marriage Act (DOMA).

- The Marriage Protection Act will remove the Supreme Court's appellate jurisdiction, as swell as remove inferior federal court original and appellate jurisdiction over DOMA's full faith and credit provision. This provision in DOMA codified that no State would be required to give full faith and credit to a marriage license issued by another State, if that relationship was between two people of the same sex.

- The Marriage Protection Act also removes appellate jurisdiction from the Supreme Court and the inferior federal courts over DOMA's marriage definition provision, which defines the terms "marriage" and "spouse," for purposes of federal law as terms only applying to relationships between people of the opposite sex.

What it Means

- This bill preserves each State's traditional right to determine its own marriage policies by preventing the federal courts from interfering with DOMA's full faith & credit provision (consistent with the 10th Amendment to the U.S. Constitution).

- Under the Marriage Protection Act, any question pertaining to the interpretation of DOMA's full faith & credit provision would be left to State courts and legislatures, where marriage law jurisdiction has traditionally resided (consistent with Article IV, Section 1 of the U.S. Constitution).

- Under the Marriage Protection Act, any question pertaining to the interpretation of DOMA's marriage definition provision could reach no higher than federal district court.

- Federal judges and Supreme Court Justices are not the elected representatives of the people, and the Marriage Protection Act will prevent federal courts from overstepping their duties and legislating from the bench regarding marriage policy.

- Congress has a constitutional duty and authority to put a check on the Judicial branch. In light of recent federal court decisions that do not respect traditional areas of law reserved for the states, the federal courts could be only one decision away from creating a "right" to homosexual marriage (consistent with Article I, Section 8, and Article III, Sections 1 & 2 of the U.S. Constitution).

BACKGROUND

- Congress passed the Defense of Marriage Act in 1996 for two reasons: 1) to defend the institution of traditional heterosexual marriage; and 2) to protect the right of the States to formulate their own public policy regarding same-sex unions, free from any federal constitutional implications that might go with one of those States creating a right for homosexual couples to acquire marriage licenses.

- DOMA has two provisions. First, Congress used its Constitutional power under the Full Faith & Credit Clause of Article IV, Section 1 of the U.S. Constitution, to provide that no State shall be required to accord full faith and credit to a marriage license issued by another State if it relates to a relationship between persons of the same sex.

- Second, DOMA defines the terms 'marriage' and 'spouse,' for purposes of federal law as terms exclusively applying to relationships between persons of the opposite sex.

- DOMA passed the House in July 1996 by a vote of 342-67, passed the Senate 85-14, and was signed into law by President Clinton in September 1996.

- This year, the Supreme Court ruled in *Lawrence v. Texas* that the Texas state sodomy law was unconstitutional because it found a "right" for individuals to engage in this kind of homosexual activity within the liberty interest of due process clause of the U.S. Constitution's 14th Amendment.

- The Supreme Court's majority opinion in *Lawrence* also insinuated, through their adherence to the law and dicta of *foreign nations*, that they might also find homosexual marriage to be a fundamental right under the liberty interest of the 14th Amendment's due process clause.

- Another case is pending in Massachusetts' state supreme court, in which it is anticipated that the court will explicitly affirm a right to homosexual marriage.

- There are many other examples of an activist judiciary out of control, such as the 9th Circuit's Pledge of Allegiance case and the 11th Circuit's 10 Commandments case–both of which Congress condemned with significant bipartisan majorities.

- Simply put, traditional heterosexual marriage is under assault by an overreaching and oligarchic judiciary. Federal DOMA will likely be a target as the federal judiciary wages war against traditional marriage.

CONCLUSION

- We cannot be passive in light of an orchestrated legal campaign to redefine the institution of marriage through the judicial process.

- DOMA was a modest effort to combat that agenda. Given the aggressive nature of the activist courts, the Marriage Protection Act puts a preemptive check on the Supreme Court and inferior federal courts by stripping their jurisdiction and preventing them from hearing any question on the full faith & credit provision of DOMA.

- The Marriage Protection Act: (1) defends and protects the institution of traditional, heterosexual marriage; (2) protects state sovereignty and self-governance; and (3) preserves scarce government resources.

- Congress must consider every Constitutional mechanism available to address the growing problem of judicial activism, and do all we can to prevent the courts from creating a new "right" by dictating to America that homosexual marriage is the supreme law of the land.

- Urge your Member of Congress to cosponsor Rep. Hostettler's Marriage Protection Act.

THE JUDICIAL SUPREMACY MYTH

- The Constitution clearly gives Congress the authority to strip jurisdiction from the federal courts. However, some are uncomfortable with this approach because, like many of us, opponents were likely instructed to believe that the Supreme Court and its decisions are the supreme law of the land.

- Today legal scholars would have you believe that in the 1803 Supreme Court case *Marbury v. Madison*, Chief Justice John Marshall forever sewed into the fabric of the American Republic that once the Supreme Court says a thing, that thing is not just the 'law of the land' but is *the supreme law of the land!*

- This notion of judicial supremacy is not supported by the U.S. Constitution or its Framers. Instead, the court imposed this authority on itself through its own decisions, most notably in *Marbury v. Madison* in 1803. But this concept was not born out in practice and did not take root in future Supreme Court decision-making, or in popular culture for that matter, until after the *Cooper v. Aaron* decision in 1958.

- Not only is that not what Marshall said in *Marbury*, but it was his belief as he related it to an associate, Justice Chase, that Congress had an 'appellate jurisdiction' over the federal judiciary.

- According to Marshall, when the Congress deemed a legal opinion of a judge to be 'unsound,' the Congress in exercising its appellate jurisdiction over the federal judiciary, would correct the situation by a 'reversal' of the 'unsound ... legal opinion.'

U.S. Supreme Court Chief Justice John Marshall 1804: Regarding the impeachment by Congress of members of the federal judiciary, Marshall wrote: "I think the modern doctrine of impeachment should yield to an appellate jurisdiction in the legislature. A reversal of those legal opinions deemed unsound by the legislature would certainly better comport with the mildness of our character than [would] a removal of the Judge who has rendered them unknowing of his fault."

Thomas Jefferson, 1820: In addition to refusing to seat Mr. Marbury, Jefferson clarified his rejection of the doctrine of judicial supremacy when he wrote: "[T]o consider the judges as the ultimate arbiters of all constitutional questions [is] a very dangerous doctrine indeed, and one which would place us under the despotism of an oligarchy. Our judges are as honest as other men, and not more so. They have, with others, the same passions for party, for power, and the privilege of their corps...[A]nd their power the more dangerous as they are in office for life, and not responsible, as the other functionaries are, to the elective control. The constitution has erected no such single tribunal."

Thomas Jefferson, 1819: "If this opinion [of judicial supremacy] be sound, then indeed is our Constitution a complete *felo de se* [act of suicide]. For intending to establish three departments, coordinate and independent, that they might check and balance one another, it has given, according to this opinion, to one of them alone the right to prescribe rules for the government of the others, and to that one, too, which is unelected by and independent of the nation... The Constitution on this hypothesis is a mere thing of wax in the hands of the judiciary, which they may twist and shape into any form they please."

Andrew Jackson, 1832: "Each public officer who takes an oath to support the Constitution swears that he will support it as he understands it, and not as it is understood by others... The opinion of judges has no more authority over Congress than the opinion of Congress had over the judges, and on that point the President is independent of both. The authority of the Supreme Court must not, therefore, be permitted to control the Congress or the Executive."

Abraham Lincoln, First Inaugural Address, 1861: "...the candid citizen must confess that if the policy of the Government upon vital questions affecting the whole people is to be irrevocably fixed by decisions of the Supreme Court the instant they are made in ordinary litigation between parties to personal actions, the people will have ceased to be their own rulers, having to that extent practically resigned their Government into the hands of that eminent tribunal."

Chapter 7

JUDICIAL ACTIVISM FORCES SAME-SEX MARRIAGE ON THE NATION[*]

Jon Kyl

SAME-SEX MARRIAGES LEGAL IN MASSACHUSETTS

A 4-3 majority of the Supreme Judicial Court of Massachusetts ruled last November in *Goodridge v. Massachusetts Dep't of Health*, 798 N.E. 2d 941 (Mass. 2003), that the state's refusal to issue marriage licenses to same-sex couples violated the state constitution. The court concluded that to insist on traditional marriage was to engage in "invidious" discrimination that the court would not tolerate. The majority, therefore, ruled that marriage must be open to same-sex couples, and delayed the decision for 180 days so that the state legislature could pass laws it "deemed necessary" in light of the decision. (*Id.* at 969-970.)

In response, the Massachusetts Senate crafted legislation to provide all the protections, benefits, and obligations of marriage to same-sex couples, but created a new parallel institution called "civil unions." This legislation would preserve traditional marriage while granting virtually all the legal benefits of marriage to same-sex couples. Because of ambiguities in the original *Goodridge* decision, the state Senate then asked the high court for its constitutional opinion of the proposed law — would civil unions that

---

[*] Excerptedf from the Republican Policy Committee July 29, 2003.

provided *all* the rights, duties, obligations, and privileges of marriage to same-sex couples satisfy the court?

The court's answer, released on February 3, was an emphatic "no." The same four-judge majority declared it would not tolerate a parallel system of "civil unions" (akin to what exists in Vermont), even though the legal arrangement would be identical to marriage itself. Thus, without any vote of the legislature or the citizens themselves, the core of the marital institution — that it shall be a union of a man and a woman — will be eliminated in Massachusetts. The only remedy the citizens of Massachusetts have for this judicial activism is a constitutional amendment process that can be completed no earlier than 2006. In the meantime, same-sex marriage licenses are expected to be issued in Massachusetts beginning on May 17.

THE MASSACHUSETTS COURT'S REJECTION OF TRADITIONAL MARRIAGE

The *Goodridge* court last November court held that "barring an individual from the protections, benefits, and obligations of civil marriage solely because that person would marry a person of the same sex violates the Massachusetts Constitution." (798 N.E. 2d at 969.) Particular highlights from the decision follow (with all emphasis added).

- Barring same-sex civil marriage "works a deep and scarring hardship on a very real segment of the community **for no rational reason.**" (*Id.* at 968.)

- Support for traditional marriage "is rooted in **persistent prejudices** against persons who are (or who are believed to be) homosexual." (*Id.*)

- There is "**no rational relationship** between the marriage statute and the Commonwealth's proffered goal of protecting the 'optimal' child-rearing unit." (*Id.* at 962.)

- "Civil marriage is an **evolving paradigm**" subject to redefinition by courts. (*Id.* at 967.)

- Defenders of traditional marriage failed "to identify **any relevant characteristic** that would justify shutting the door to civil marriage to a person who wishes to marry someone of the same sex." (*Id.* at 968.)

- "[I]t is **circular reasoning**, not analysis, to maintain that marriage must remain a heterosexual institution because that is what it historically has been." (*Id.* at 961 n.23.)

- The court's role is to **limit the influence of "historical, cultural, [and] religious ... reasons** " that the State may rely upon in attempting to preserve traditional marriage. (*Id.* at 965 n.29.)

- "The continuous maintenance of this **caste-like system** is irreconcilable with, indeed, totally repugnant to the State's strong interest in the welfare of all children and its primary focus, in the context of family law where children are concerned, on 'the best interests of the child.'" (*Id.* at 972 (Greaney, J., concurring).)

- To note the long history of traditional marriage is to rely on nothing more than a **"mantra of tradition."** (*Id.* at 973 (Greaney, J., concurring).)

Three justices dissented from the decision, arguing that only the state legislature has the authority to make such a dramatic change to the civil marriage institution, and lamenting the majority's claim that the State's opposition to same-sex marriage was irrational.

- "It is surely pertinent to the inquiry to recognize that this proffered change affects not just a load-bearing wall of our social structure but the very cornerstone of that structure." (*Id.* at 981 (Sosman, J., dissenting).)

- The majority stripped the elected representatives of their right to evaluate the "consequences of that alteration, [and] to make sure that it can be done safely, without either temporary or lasting damage to the structural integrity of the entire edifice." (*Id.* at 982 (Sosman, J., dissenting).)

- The majority justices instead imposed their will under the assumption "that there are no dangers and that it is safe to proceed, ... an assumption that is not supported by anything more than the court's blind faith that it is so." (*Id.*)

THE COURT INSISTS ON "MARRIAGE" AND REJECTS A CIVIL UNION OPTION

The Massachusetts Senate's subsequent drafting of a "civil unions" bill was designed to satisfy the court's edict while preserving traditional marriage. To ensure its constitutionality, the state Senate requested an advisory opinion from the Massachusetts court. Despite the fact that all legal rights and benefits were provided in the civil unions legislation, the court rejected this alternative legislation, insisting that marriage itself must be redefined. *Opinions of Justices to the Senate*, SJC 09163 (Feb. 3, 2004), available at www.state.ma.us/courts/opinionstothesenate.pdf. Highlights from that decision follow.

- The proposed law granting all the rights, benefits, and privileges of marriage through "civil unions" suffers from **"defects in rationality."** (*Id.* at 8.)

- "For **no rational reason**, the marriage laws of the Commonwealth discriminate against a defined class; **no amount of tinkering with language can eradicate that stain."** (*Id.* at 11.)

- "The bill would have the effect of maintaining and fostering a **stigma of exclusion** that the [Massachusetts] constitution prohibits." (*Id.* at 11.)

- Any attempt to preserve traditional marriage is little more than **"invidious discrimination."** (*Id.* at 10.)

- The court indicates that the elimination of civil marriage altogether is constitutionally preferable to the preservation of traditional marriage. (*Id.* at 11 n.4.)

In light of the court's refusal to entertain a solution that granted all benefits and privileges of marriage through civil unions, Massachusetts is expected to issue marriage licenses to same-sex couples on May 17, 2004.

HOW THE MASSACHUSETTS
DECISION AFFECTS OTHER STATES

Same-sex couples from across the United States intend to travel to Massachusetts this summer, marry, and then return to their home states to settle.[1] While Massachusetts law appears to prohibit the issuance of marriage licenses to non-resident same-sex couples who intend to return to states where such "marriages" are illegal, see Mass. G.L. 207 §§ 11-13, the fate of that law is uncertain and press reports make clear that many non-Massachusetts citizens intend to marry there and return to their home states. And Massachusetts same-sex residents who marry there can, of course, later move to other states. In both instances, those same-sex couples may seek recognition of their Massachusetts marriages in other states so that they can receive all the privileges, benefits, and rights that each state gives to married couples.

These Massachusetts marriages will serve as the gateway to additional judicial activism throughout the United States. Some same-sex couples will ally themselves with homosexual-rights activists and challenge both provisions of federal DOMA (the "Defense of Marriage Act") — 1) the section that prevents same-sex married couples from accessing federal benefits such as joint tax filing privileges, Social Security spousal payments, and federal employee spousal eligibility, and 2) the section that bolsters the ability of states to refuse recognition of out-of-state same-sex marriages. Other activists will follow the Massachusetts model and demand that state supreme courts redefine marriage by judicial fiat, as plaintiffs have urged recently in New Jersey, Arizona, Indiana, Alaska, Hawaii, and Vermont.[2]

---

[1] The press reports that Massachusetts wedding planners and town clerks are fielding calls "from as far away as Alaska and Hawaii" from same-sex couples who intend to marry this summer in Massachusetts. Thomas Caywood, "Clerks getting pre-wedding jitters," *Boston Herald*, 6 Feb. 2004. See also articles discussing American same-sex couples marrying in Canada and returning to United States to live. *E.g.*, Sarah Robertson, "Mining the Gold in Gay Nuptials," *New York Times*, 19 Dec. 2003.

[2] See *Lewis v. Harris*, No. MER-L-03, 2003 WL 2319114 (N.J. Super. L. Nov. 5, 2003) (denying plaintiffs' demand for marriage license; case now pending appeal); *Standhardt v. Superior Court*, 77 P.3d 451 (Ariz. App. 2003) (affirming denial of marriage license to plaintiffs; case pending petition to Arizona Supreme Court); *Morrison v. Stadler*, No. 49D13-0211-PL 001946 (Marion County (Indiana) Super. Ct.) (relief denied to plaintiff; on appeal to Indiana Court of Appeals); *Brause v. State, Dep't of Health*, 21 P.3d 357 (Alaska 2001) (affirming dismissal on mootness grounds due to state constitutional amendment barring same-sex marriage recognition); *Baehr v. Miike*, 1996 WL 694235 (Hawaii Cir. Ct.

As these activist-driven state court cases are filed, they will confront resistance in the 38 states that have passed some form of a "State DOMA" that enshrines in state law support for traditional marriage.

States with "DOMAs"
(constitutional amendments marked with *)

Alabama	Georgia	Louisiana	Nevada*	Tennessee
Alaska*	Hawaii*	Maine	North Carolina	Texas
Arizona	Idaho	Michigan	North Dakota	Utah
Arkansas	Illinois	Minnesota	Ohio	Virginia
California	Indiana	Mississippi	Oklahoma	Washington
Colorado	Iowa	Missouri	Pennsylvania	West Virginia
Delaware	Kansas	Montana	South Carolina	
Florida	Kentucky	Nebraska*	South Dakota	

Only Alaska, Hawaii, Nebraska, and Nevada have state constitutional amendments that prevent a state supreme court from ruling these "State DOMAs" unconstitutional. And, of course, no State DOMA can prevent a federal court from striking down a state constitutional amendment under federal constitutional standards. (The Nebraska state constitutional amendment has been challenged in federal court and is now awaiting trial. Citizens for Equal Protection, Inc. v. Bruning, 290 F. Supp. 2d 1004 (2003).) So far, state court lawsuits are pending in Arizona, Indiana, and New Jersey, each of which asks the state courts to rule that the state constitutional equal protection and/or due process provisions require imposition of same-sex marriage.

Many same-sex couples do not wish to be litigious, but it is inevitable that many of them will challenge state marriage laws through the regular course of living in their home states. For example, courts in Texas, Iowa, and New York have already confronted cases addressing the reach of Vermont civil unions in the case of "divorces" and the right to sue on behalf of a deceased "spouse."[3] Thus, while the conscious campaign for judicial

---

Dec. 3, 1996) (superseded by constitutional amendment); *Baker v. State*, 744 A.2d 864 (Vt. 1999) (causing legislature to enact civil unions law).

[3] The unpublished Texas decision relating to dissolution of a Vermont civil union (which was later reconsidered) is discussed at http://www.washtimes.com/national/20031215-110146-5298r.htm. The Iowa decision regarding the same, also reconsidered, is discussed at http://desmoinesregister.com/news/stories/c4788993/22995747.html. The full text of the New York decision regarding the right to sue as a surviving spouse if one is in a Vermont

imposition of same-sex marriage through the courts is well documented,[4] that campaign ultimately may pale in comparison to the opportunities for judicial activism that will arise when same-sex couples settle in states where their marriages are not recognized.

CONCLUSION

President Bush said in his State of the Union address, "If judges insist on forcing their arbitrary will upon the people, the only alternative left to the people would be the constitutional process." That constitutional process begins when each house of Congress proposes a constitutional amendment and presents it to the American people for ratification through their state legislatures.[5] The recent judicial activism in Massachusetts, especially when seen in the context of the ongoing campaign in the courts, would certainly justify the Judiciary Committee holding hearings on the propriety of proposing an appropriate constitutional amendment. Ultimately, the future of marriage should be decided by the American people, not by activist courts.

---

civil union is available at http://www.marriagewatch.org/cases/ny/langan/trial/sj_opinion. pdf.

[4] See, for example, Senate Republican Policy Committee, "The Threat to Marriage from the Courts" (July 29, 2003), available at http://rpc.senate.gov/releases/2003/jd072903.pdf.

[5] U.S. Constitution, art. V.

Chapter 8

THE FEDERAL INCOME TAX AND THE TREATMENT OF MARRIED COUPLES: BACKGROUND AND ANALYSIS[*]

Gregg A. Esenwein

INTRODUCTION

Defining the married couple as a single tax unit under the federal individual income tax tends to violates the principle of marriage neutrality. Marriage neutrality means that the tax system should not influence the choice of individuals with regard to their marital status. However, under the current federal income tax system, some married couples pay more income tax than they would as two unmarried singles (a marriage tax penalty) while other married couples pay less income tax than they would as two unmarried singles (a marriage tax bonus).

A marriage neutral income tax, however, is an elusive goal. Marriage neutrality conflicts with two other concepts of equity: progressivity and equal taxation of couples with equal incomes. Regardless of how these three concepts of equity are juggled, an income tax can achieve any two of these goals but cannot simultaneously achieve all three.

---

[*] Excerpted from CRS Report RL30800.

Since its inception in 1913, Congress has repeatedly modified the federal income tax and has switched emphasis among these three goals. Originally, the federal income tax was marriage neutral but did not tax couples with equal incomes equally. Later it emphasized the equal taxation of couples with similar incomes but achieved this result at the expense of marriage neutrality. Other modifications have involved trade-offs between increased marriage neutrality and structural progressivity.

Given the possibility of tax legislation in the 107th Congress that might affect the marriage neutrality of the individual income tax, the remainder of this report provides background information and analysis of the issues associated with the federal individual income tax and marriage neutrality.[1] Issues addressed include a discussion of the conflicting goals of equity under an income tax, an explanation of the causes of structural marriage penalties and bonuses, an overview of the historical tax treatment of marital status, an analysis of the income splits that produce structural marriage penalties and bonuses, estimates of the magnitude of structural penalties and bonuses at various income levels, and a brief examination of possible legislative solutions.

CONFLICTING GOALS OF EQUITY UNDER AN INCOME TAX

A widely accepted goal is that the individual income tax should be marriage neutral. Marriage neutrality means that the tax system should not influence the choice of individuals with regard to their marital status. That is, a couple's combined federal income tax liability should be the same if they are married or if they are single.

Marriage neutrality, however, tends to conflict with two other concepts of equity: that the tax system should be progressive (income tax payments should rise as a percentage of income as incomes increase) and that couples with the same total incomes should pay the same amount of income tax.

To appreciate the mutual exclusivity of these three goals of equity consider the following illustration (an algebraic representation of this

---

[1] Legislative proposals affecting the marriage neutrality of the income tax have the potential of causing unintended interactions with the alternative minimum tax for individuals. For more information on this issue see CRS Report RL30485, *The Individual Alternative Minimum Tax: Interaction with Marriage Penalty Relief and Other Tax Cuts*, by Jane G. Gravelle.

example is contained in the appendix). Assume that there are four individuals: Andy, Betty, Cathy, and David. Andy and Betty each earn incomes of $30,000 while David's income is $60,000. Cathy has no income at all.

If the tax system is progressive, then David who has $60,000 of income, should pay a higher tax than the combined tax of Andy and Betty, who only have incomes of $30,000 each. On the other hand, if the tax system were proportional, then the combined income tax of Andy and Betty would equal the income tax on David. (Alternatively, if the tax system were regressive, then the combined tax of Andy and Betty would be greater than David's tax.)

Now consider what would happen if Andy and Betty got married and David and Cathy got married. If the tax system is marriage neutral, then the tax on Andy and Betty as a married couple should be the same as their combined income tax as two single individuals. Likewise, as a married couple, David and Cathy should pay the same amount of income tax as combined income tax they paid while they were single.

The third concept of equity requires that couples with the same incomes pay the same amount of income tax. In this case, Andy and Betty who have a $60,000 income and Cathy and David, who also have $60,000 of income should pay the same amount of income tax.

However, it is obvious that if these two couples pay the same amount of income tax, then the tax system cannot be progressive, since the combined tax of Andy and Betty is now the same as income tax paid solely by David on his $60,000 income. In this case the tax system is proportional (David pays the same amount of tax as the combined tax of Andy and Betty) rather than progressive (David would pay a larger amount of tax than the combined tax of Andy and Betty).

Regardless of how these three concepts of equity are juggled, under current definitions an income tax can be designed to achieve any two of these goals, but it cannot simultaneously achieve all three. The system might be marriage neutral and tax couples with equal incomes equally but it could not be progressive. As an alternative, the tax system might be progressive and tax couples with equal incomes equally but then it would not be marriage neutral. Finally, the tax system could be progressive and marriage neutral but not tax couples with equal incomes equally. The current federal income tax system has chosen progressivity and equal taxation of couples with equal incomes at the expense of marriage neutrality.

These three goals of equity are not mutually exclusive if the definition of what constitutes equal couples is modified. For instance, the equity argument for equal taxation of couples with the same total income is weaker when the comparison is between two-earner married couples and one-earner married couples. Economics recognizes that in this case the couples are, in fact, not equal since the one-earner couple benefits from the extra time available to the non-working spouse, a benefit not available to the two-earner couple.

If the economic distinction between one-earner and two-earner couples as it relates to the principle of equal taxation of couples with equal incomes is accepted, then the three concepts of equity are not necessarily in conflict. Hence, by redefining what constitutes equal couples, the income tax system can be progressive, marriage neutral, and tax couples with equal incomes and circumstances equally.

However, the practical difficulties of including both incomes and circumstances in the definition of equality between couples would be significant. For instance, while the case of a two-earner versus one-earner couple is fairly straightforward, the case is not so clear for couples under other circumstances. How would the tax system account for circumstances when a two-earner couple has the same income as a couple with one full-time and one part-time worker? Using measures other than income to define equality between couples might invite more dissatisfaction than the current system.

CAUSES OF STRUCTURAL PENALTIES AND BONUSES

The three most important structural features affecting the marriage neutrality of the income tax are the earned income tax credit (EITC), the standard deduction, and the tax rate schedules. Under the current income tax system, single individuals, heads of households, and married couples are subject to different standard deductions and tax rate schedules. The EITC amounts and phaseout ranges also vary according to filing status. These differences give rise to structural marriage tax penalties and bonuses.

For example, consider the standard deductions for joint and single returns in 2000. The standard deduction is $7,350 for joint returns and $4,400 for single returns. Hence, two singles get a combined standard deduction of $8,400 compared to $7,350 as a joint return. To be completely marriage neutral, the joint standard deduction should be twice the amount of the single standard deduction. The structural asymmetry also appears in the marginal tax rate brackets where the joint return marginal tax rate brackets are not exactly twice the width of the marginal tax rate brackets for single returns. (A table containing the tax rate brackets and standard deductions for tax year 2000 in contained in appendix B.)

Because of these asymmetries, when the income of one spouse is added to the income of the other spouse, a married couple might find themselves paying either more federal income tax (a marriage penalty) or less tax (a marriage bonus) than they would by filing as two singles. Conversely, two singles (or some combination of singles and heads of households) contemplating marriage might find that their federal income tax liability increases (a marriage tax penalty) or decreases (a marriage tax bonus) by filing a joint return.

Others features of the federal individual income tax system that have the potential of affecting the marriage neutrality of the system include, among others, the tax treatment of Social Security benefits, the child care tax credit, the additional standard deductions for the elderly and the blind, the net capital loss offset, limits on the tax-free gain from the sale of a principal residence by a taxpayer aged 55 years or older, and limits on deferred compensation plans.[2]

In general, the division of income, or income split, of the two individuals determines whether they will have a marriage tax bonus or penalty. The largest marriage tax bonuses occur when one spouse earns 100% of the income. In this case, the married couple can take full advantage of the higher standard deduction and the lower marginal tax rate brackets for joint returns. Had they filed as two singles, since only one had income, the entire tax burden would have been borne by the one individual filing a single return.

The more evenly divided the income the more likely a married couple will experience a marriage tax penalty. The largest tax penalties occur where the income is evenly divided between the two spouses, a 50/50 income split. In this instance the stacking of income and the resultant taxation at higher marginal tax rates produces a larger income tax liability for a joint return than would have been the case for two single returns. At the lower end of the income scale, the joining of incomes may produce a reduced EITC for joint returns compared to what they would have had if the couple had filed as two singles (or heads of households).

---

[2] A comprehensive list of the income tax provisions that affect the marriage neutrality of the federal income tax can be found in: U.S. Congress. General Accounting Office. *Income Tax Treatment of Married and Single Individuals*. GAO/GDD 96-175. September 1996.

HISTORICAL TAX TREATMENT OF MARITAL STATUS

The fact that the federal individual income tax system can produce marriage tax penalties and bonuses has long been recognized. When the individual income tax was originally enacted in 1913, married couples were required to file separate returns if each spouse had income. In fact, married couples could minimize their total federal income tax burden by evenly splitting their income when they filed their separate returns.

This system gave married couples in community property states an advantage over married couples in common law states. Regardless of which spouse earned the income, couples in community property states were able to split their income 50/50 for federal income tax purposes. Married couples in common law states, however, were required to divide their income according to which spouse actually earned the income. Married couples in community property states continued to enjoy the advantage of income splitting through 1947. Hence, the federal income tax system was progressive and marriage neutral but it did not tax couples with equal incomes equally. (Couples who lived in community property states had lower federal income tax liabilities than couples with the same incomes who lived in common property law states.)

The Revenue Act of 1948 effectively extended the benefits of income splitting to all married couples, including those who lived in common law states. The 1948 Act changed the federal income tax rate brackets so that, in effect, married couples were taxed as two singles. There were now two tax rate schedules: one for married couples filing joint returns and one for individuals filing single returns. The change in tax rate structures, while alleviating the dichotomy in the taxation of married couples living in community and common law property states, significantly increased the tax burden of single individuals relative to married couples. Single individuals paid considerably more in federal income taxes than did married couples at the same income level. Thus, the Revenue Act of 1948 emphasized more equal taxation of couples with equal incomes at the expense of marital neutrality. (Singles could reduce their income tax liability by getting married; hence, the reciprocal of a single's tax penalty is a marriage tax bonus).

The Tax Reform Act of 1969 addressed this problem of the single's tax penalty by reducing the tax rate schedule of single returns relative to the tax rate schedule for joint returns. In general, the tax rate reductions for single returns were designed so that over the middle income ranges the tax liability of a single return would be no more than 20% higher than the tax liability of a married couple with the same income filing a joint return. Although reducing the single's tax penalty, the Tax Reform Act of 1969 meant that some two-earner married couples paid more in federal income tax (a marriage tax penalty) filing a joint return than they would have if they filed as two singles, while others paid less (a marriage bonus). Hence, the 1969 Act merely rearranged the lack of marriage neutrality under the federal income tax.

The Economic Recovery Tax Act of 1981 contained provisions which were designed to reduce the problem of marriage tax penalties. Under this Act, two-earner married couples were allowed to reduce their taxable income by an amount equal to 10% of the lower-earning spouse's earned income (the maximum reduction in taxable income was $2,000). This two-earner marital deduction helped to reduce the marriage tax penalties faced by some two-earner married couples, but it did not eliminate the penalties for all couples. Moreover, for some two-earner married couples, the provision actually increased their marriage tax bonuses. In the attempt to make the income tax system more marriage neutral, the two-earner deduction introduced a violation of the principle of equal taxation of couples with equal incomes (two-earner couples would pay less income tax than one-earner couples with the same income).

The Tax Reform Act of 1986 changed the tax rate brackets and the standard deductions for both single and joint returns. Tax rates were substantially lowered and the number of statutory marginal tax rates were reduced from 14 to two. In addition, the standard deduction for joint returns was increased proportionally more than the standard deduction for single returns.

It was argued that the change in the relationship between the standard deductions for joint and single returns along with the flattening out of the tax rate structure reduced the need for the two-earner marital deduction. As a consequence, the two-earner marital deduction was repealed.

At the same time, however, the 1986 Act also introduced new marital-specific provisions governing contributions to individual retirement accounts (IRAs) for workers covered by employee-sponsored pension plans. The Act also contained provisions establishing additions to the standard deductions of the elderly and blind, the size of which were a function of marital status.

Thus, on the one hand, the 1986 Act increased the marriage neutrality of the federal income tax by reducing its structural progressivity (through a flattening of the rate structure) while it simultaneously made the system less marriage neutral by introducing new marital specific tax provisions.

The Omnibus Budget Reconciliation Act of 1990 (OBRA90) also affected the marriage neutrality of the federal income tax. It did so primarily through a change in the marginal income tax rate schedule. OBRA90 legislated a new 31% marginal tax rate and thus created a 3-tiered statutory marginal tax rate structure as opposed to the 2-tiered statutory rate structure under prior law.

More significant changes affecting the marriage neutrality of the federal income tax occurred with the passage of the Omnibus Budget Reconciliation Act of 1993 (OBRA93). OBRA93 made two major structural changes that had ramifications for marriage neutrality. It increased and expanded the EITC, and it added two new marginal tax rates, 36% and 39.6%, at the upper end of the income scale.

The EITC was changed in several ways. OBRA93 repealed the supplemental tax credit for children under one year of age and the supplemental tax credit for health insurance premiums for children. At the same time, OBRA93 increased the maximum EITC for families with qualifying children; extended the income ranges over which the EITC is phased out; and extended EITC coverage to childless taxpayers ages 25 to 64 who are not claimed as dependents on another taxpayer's return.

By increasing the EITC and adding two new tax brackets at the upper-end of the income scale, OBRA93 increased the structural progressivity of the individual income tax. The cost of the increased structural progessivity, however, was a decrease in the marriage neutrality of the federal income tax over these two income ranges.

The 104th Congress addressed the issue of the marriage neutrality of the federal income tax as part of the Balanced Budget Act of 1995. The House version of the Act included a provision which would have provided a nonrefundable credit of up to $145 as a means of relieving the marriage tax penalties of certain two-earner married couples. The Senate opted for a different approach and included a provision which would have increased the standard deduction for joint returns relative to the standard deduction for single returns. The Conference agreement followed the Senate approach and modified the standard deduction for joint returns such that, by the year 2005 and there after, it would be twice the size of the standard deduction for single returns. The Balanced Budget Act of 1995, however, was ultimately vetoed by President Clinton.

Several marriage tax penalty relief bills were also introduced during the 105th Congress. These bills took multiple forms including proposals for two-earner marital deductions, proposals to increase the standard deduction for joint returns, and proposals to widen the tax brackets for joint returns to twice the width of the tax brackets for single returns. However, marriage penalty tax relief did not end up in the final tax cut package, the Taxpayer Relief Act of 1997 (P.L. 105-34), which was signed into law on August 5, 1997.

Marriage penalty tax relief was a major legislative issue in the 106th Congress. The Marriage Penalty Tax Relief Reconciliation Act of 2000 (H.R. 4810) was passed by the House on July 20, 2000 and by the Senate on July 21, 2000. It would have increased the standard deduction for joint returns to twice the size of the standard deduction for single returns, increased the width of the 15% tax bracket for joint returns to twice the width of the 15% tax bracket for single returns, and would have increased the phaseout point for the EITC by $2,000 for married couples. President Clinton citing revenue and distributional concerns vetoed H.R. 4810 in August 2000.[3]

Marriage penalty tax relief is a subject of legislative activity in the 107th Congress. President George W. Bush included a proposal for a two-earner marital deduction as part of his across-the-board tax cut plan. In late March 2001, the House passed H.R. 6 which contained marriage penalty tax relief provisions.

MEASURING THE EXTENT AND AMOUNT OF MARRIAGE TAX PENALTIES AND BONUSES

Significant practical problems are associated with actually defining and measuring the extent of marriage tax bonuses and penalties. The first issue involves deciding on the appropriate basis of comparison. Should marriage tax penalties and bonuses be computed on the basis of how the tax liabilities of two singles would change if they got married? Or should the basis of comparison be the change in tax liability that would occur if a married couple could file as two single individuals?

---

[3] For more information on legislation in the 106th Congress see CRS Report RL30420, *Marriage Tax Penalties: Legislative Proposals in the 106th Congress*, by Gregg A. Esenwein.

Each of these approaches present problems. Both the Congressional Budget Office (CBO) and the Treasury Department have opted for computing marriage tax penalties and bonuses by taking married couples and computing their tax liabilities as if they were single. However, this approach necessitates making difficult assumptions about how children, income, and deductions should be allocated between two spouses.

For instance, when a married couple has children how do you allocate the children when calculating marriage tax penalties and bonuses? If there is only one child, who should get to claim the child as a dependent? For purposes of calculating marriage tax penalties and bonuses should the spouse claiming the child be allowed to file as a head of household? If there are two or more children should each parent be allocated children and thus both be eligible for filing as head of household?

Also problematic is the inclusion and allocation of unearned income. How do you divide unearned income between spouses, do you give the unearned income to the lower earning spouse or to the higher earning spouse? Should you allocate the unearned income based on the ratio of the spouses' earned income? The treatment of itemized deductions presents a similar quandary. How should the deductions be allocated between the two spouses?

In its most recent estimates, CBO offers two alternative measures of marriage tax bonuses and penalties. In its basic measure CBO assumes that all unearned income is allocated to each spouse in proportion to their earned income. Itemized deductions are allocated on the same basis. If there is one child, then the higherearning spouse claims the dependent and files as a head of household. If there are two or more children, then the lower-earning spouse claims one dependent and files as a head of household while the higher-earning spouse claims the other children as dependents and also files as a head of household.[4]

Under this approach, which could be considered a tax minimization approach, in 1999, 43% of all married couples were estimated to have marriage tax penalties with aggregate penalties amounting to $32 billion. Some 52% of married couples were estimated to have marriage tax bonuses with aggregate bonuses totaling $42 billion. The remaining 5% of married couples were unaffected. Under this measure, there was a net marriage tax bonus of $10 billion.

---

[4] U.S. Congress. Congressional Budget Office. *Updated Estimates of Marriage Penalties and Bonuses.* Memorandum dated September 18, 1998.

CBO's alternative measure assigned all children to the lower-earning spouse, a measure which they refer to as a "divorce model". Under this measure in 1999, 37% of married couples had a marriage tax penalty with penalties amounting to $24 billion. An estimated 60% of couples had a marriage tax bonus with total bonuses of $73 billion. The remaining 3% of couples were unaffected. Under this divorce model there was a net marriage tax bonus of $49 billion.

The Office of Tax Analysis (OTA) at the Treasury Department uses a resource pooling approach to estimate marriage tax penalties and bonuses. This approach is based on the assumption that married couples could maintain the same living and financial arrangements that occurs within the marriage without actually being married. Under this approach, the higher-earning spouse is assumed to claim head of household status and take all personal exemptions for dependents. All deductions associated with dependents and maintenance of the household are also claimed by the higher-earning spouse. Unearned income is allocated in proportion to earned income.[5]

Using this resource pooling methodology OTA estimated that in 1999, 48% of married couples incurred a marriage tax penalty, 41% had a marriage tax bonus, and the remaining 11% were unaffected. Aggregate marriage tax penalties are estimated at $28.3 billion, aggregate marriage tax bonuses were estimated at $26.7 billion for a net marriage tax penalty in 1999 of $1.6 billion.

The CBO and OTA estimates of marriage tax penalties and bonuses for 1999 are summarized in the following table.

---

[5] U.S. Department of the Treasury. *Defining and Measuring Marriage Penalties and Bonuses.* By Nicholas Bull, Janet Holtzblatt, and James R. Nunns. November 1999.

Table 1. Estimates of Aggregate Tax Penalties and Bonuses for 1999

	CBO Estimates		OTA Estimates
	Basic Model	Divorce Model	Resource Pooling Model
Married Couples with Marriage Tax Penalties:			
Percent of total	43%	37%	48%
Aggregate $ amount (billions)	$32	$24	$28.3
Married Couples with Marriage Tax Bonuses:			
Percent of total	52%	60%	41%
Aggregate $ amount (billions)	$42	$73	$26.7
Married Couples Unaffected:			
Percent of total	5%	3%	11%
Net Aggregate Penalty or (Bonuses)	($10)	($49)	$1.6

The difficulties of accurately defining and measuring marriage tax penalties and bonuses cannot be over stressed.[6] From a theoretical perspective it is not even clear what the appropriate base line comparison should be: should it be the tax consequences if two single individuals decide to marry or, should it be the tax consequences if a married couple were allowed to file as two separate individuals? Furthermore, the basic economic characteristics of married couples, heads of households and single individuals are different. As a result, including children, unearned income, and itemized deductions into the calculations can introduce measurement errors that reflect these basic differences in the economic characteristics of the filing units rather than the marriage tax penalties and bonuses that arise because of the structural components of the tax system.

To avoid these measurement problems the remainder of this report will concentrate on the "structural" marriage tax bonuses and penalties in the federal income tax system. Comparisons will be based on earned income only and will exclude head of household status, unearned income, dependents, and itemized deductions.

---

[6] For more information on the problems of measuring marriage tax penalties and bonuses see CRS Report RL30419, *The Marriage Tax Penalty: An Overview of the Issues*, by Jane G. Gravelle

Income Splits That Produce
Structural Penalties and Bonuses

As mentioned earlier, it is principally the EITC, differences in the standard deductions, and differences between the tax rate schedules for joint and single returns that gives rise to structural marriage tax penalties and bonuses. When the income of one spouse is added to the income of the other spouse, married couples may find that they pay more in income tax (marriage tax penalty) or less in income tax (marriage tax bonus) than they would if they had filed as two singles. The division of income, or income split, of the two spouses determines whether they have a bonus or penalty.

The largest marriage bonuses occur when one spouse earns 100% of the total income. In this case, the married couple can take full advantage of the larger standard deduction and lower marginal tax rate brackets for joint returns. Had they filed as two singles, since one spouse had no income, the entire tax would have been borne by one individual filing a single return. Under these circumstances, because of the differences in EITCs, standard deductions, and tax rate brackets, the couple would pay far less income tax by filing a joint return than they would have by filing a single return.

Conversely, the more evenly divided the income, the more likely a married couple will experience a marriage tax penalty. Indeed, the largest marriage tax penalties occur where the income is evenly divided between the two spouses, a 50/50 income split. In this instance, the asymmetry between standard deductions for joint and single returns and the stacking of income which results in taxation at higher marginal income tax rates produces higher income tax liabilities for the couple filing a joint return than would be the case had they filed as two singles.

Between these two points, there is a specific income split that would produce no marriage tax penalty or bonus. In other words, at this break-even income split, the tax code would be essentially marriage neutral since a married couple would pay the same in income taxes by filing a joint return or by filing two single returns. These break-even income splits are shown in table 2.

This table shows for each specific income level the income division between the two spouse that would produce neither marriage tax penalties nor marriage tax bonuses. For example, at the $40,000 income level, a married couple with one spouse earning 88% of the income and the other earning 12% of the income would pay the same income tax whether they file a joint return or two single returns. If they file a joint return, then their federal income tax would be $4,058. If they file two single returns, then the federal income tax on the spouse with the higher income ($35,140) would be $4,411 while the lower earning spouse ($5,774) would receive an EITC of $353, for a total tax of $4,058.

If the couple's income is more evenly divided than the break-even income splits shown in the table, then they will experience a marriage tax penalty. If their income is less evenly divided than that shown in the table, then they will experience a marriage tax bonus. For instance, a couple earning $40,000 with an income split of 70/30 would experience a marriage tax penalty. If the couple's income were split 90/10, then they would experience a marriage tax bonus.

Table 2. Break-Even Income Splits Income Splits That Produce Neither Marriage Tax Penalties Nor Bonuses Tax Year 2000

Total Income	Income Earned by each Spouse		Percentage of Total Earned by each Spouse	
(1)	(2)	(3)	(4)	(5)
$20,000	$16,194	$3,806	81%	19%
$30,000	$26,194	$3,806	87%	13%
$40,000	$35,140	$4,860	88%	12%
$50,000	$35,123	$14,877	70%	30%
$70,000	$48,323	$21,677	69%	31%
$100,000	$76,900	$23,100	77%	23%
$150,000	$123,356	$26,644	82%	18%
$250,000	$222,235	$27,765	89%	11%
$500,000	$479,310	$20,690	96%	4%

Source: Calculated by CRS. Assumes all earned income and use of standard deduction.

Amount of Structural Penalties and Bonuses

This section of the report examines the structural marriage tax penalties and bonuses that occur at selected income levels between $20,000 and $500,000. The federal income tax liabilities of married couples with various income splits filing joint returns were calculated and then compared to the combined tax liability if they had filed as two single individuals. Taxes were calculated for tax year 2000 and were based on the assumption that all income was earned income and that the standard deduction was used. Over the appropriate lower income levels, use of the EITC was also included.

Table 3 shows the structural marriage tax penalties and bonuses measured as the dollar amount by which the income tax liability on the joint return is different from that of the combined tax liability on the two single returns. Marriage tax bonuses are shown in parentheses.

For example, table 3 shows that a married couple with $50,000 of income and a 50/50 income split would pay $218 more in federal income taxes by filing a joint return than they would have had they been able to file as two single individuals. For married couples whose income is all taxed in the 15% tax bracket, the maximum structural marriage tax penalty is $218. This is simply 15% of the difference between the standard deduction for a joint return, $7,350, and the combined total, $8800, of two standard deductions (at $4,400 each) for single returns. In dollar terms, the largest marriage tax penalties occur at the upper-end of the income spectrum. For instance, the structural marriage tax penalty for a couple earning $500,000 with a 50/50 income split is almost $15,000.

On the other hand, the largest relative marriage tax penalties actually occur in the $20,000 to $25,000 income range. Contrary to the general rule of the largest penalties occurring when income is more evenly split, in this income range marriage tax penalties are larger for married couples with income splits of 60/40 and 70/30 then for the couples with 50/50 income splits. The reason for this result is that the EITC would be available for the lower earning spouse at these income splits if the married couple were allowed to file as two singles. Where the income is more evenly divided, both spouses would have incomes that would exceed the limit for qualification for the EITC.

Table 3. Structural Marriage Tax Penalties and Bonuses in 2000
(Assuming all earned income and use of the standard deduction)

Total Income	Income Taxes if Filing Jointly	Tax Penalties and Bonuses (Tax Bonuses shown in parentheses)			
		If income is split between the spouses:			
		50/50	60/40	70/30	100/0
$20,000	$1,058	$276	$400	$373	($862)
$30,000	$2,558	$218	$218	$324	($862)
$40,000	$4,058	$218	$218	$218	($1,714)
$50,000	$5,558	$218	$218	$16	($3,014)
$75,000	$11,674	$1,530	$1,082	$107	($4,026)
$100,000	$18,674	$1,530	$1,530	$1,082	($4,776)
$150,000	$33,607	$2,208	$1,885	$1,435	($6,033)
$250,000	$69,314	$6,915	$6,224	$4,772	($7,133)
$500,000	$167,758	$14,864	$14,986	$13,590	($6,170)

Calculated by CRS

Table 3 clearly shows that, for all but the highest income levels, marriage tax bonuses are far larger than marriage tax penalties. For example, while the maximum marriage tax penalty for a $50,000 household is $218, the maximum marriage tax bonus is $3,014.

Possible Legislative Solutions

As pointed out earlier in this report, making the federal income tax marriage neutral while maintaining the other two equity goals of progressivity and equal taxation of couples with equal incomes is an impossible task. The major legislative solutions involve some form of compromise between these three equity principles. The four main legislative approaches in the past have been a second-earner marital deduction, separate filing, increasing the standard deduction and tax rate brackets for joint returns, and increasing the standard deduction for joint returns. These approaches are briefly discussed below.

Second-Earner Deduction

A second-earner deduction would allow the lower-earning spouse to deduct a percentage of his/her earned income (wage and salary income) from the couple's taxable income base. This approach was used in the federal income tax between 1981 and 1986. The Economic Recovery Tax Act of 1981 contained second-earner deduction provisions designed to reduce marriage tax penalties. Under the Act, two-earner married couples were allowed to reduce their taxable income by an amount equal to 10% of the lower earning spouse's earned income. The maximum deduction was $2,000. This second earner marital deduction was repealed in the Tax Reform Act of 1986.

A second-earner deduction would eliminate marriage tax penalties for some couples, reduce penalties for other couples, and increase or produce marriage tax bonuses for yet other couples. This approach fails to achieve the equity principle that couples with the same total income should pay the same amount of federal income tax. It is, however, one of the least expensive legislative options.

Optional Separate Filing

Optional separate filing would allow married couples the option to file as two single taxpayers rather than file a joint return as a married couple. As the name implies, this option would allow married couples to file as two single individuals on the same return or to continue to file a joint return, the decision being based on which option produced the lowest income tax liability.

In general, optional separate filing would mean that couples who currently incur marriage tax penalties could, by filing as two singles, eliminate their marriage tax penalties. Couples who currently have marriage tax bonuses could continue to file joint returns and thus would see no change in their federal income tax liabilities. Although eliminating marriage tax penalties, this option would not make the federal income tax marriage neutral since it would maintain marriage tax bonuses. Hence, this approach would fail to achieve the equity goal that married couples with similar incomes pay similar amounts of federal income tax. The differences in income tax liabilities between couples with similar incomes could be much larger than they would be under a second-earner deduction approach.

Increasing the Standard Deduction and
Tax Rate Brackets for Joint Returns

Another major legislative approach to solving the marriage tax penalty problem would be to increase the standard deduction and width of the tax rate brackets for joint returns to twice that of single returns. An alternative approach, but one that has the same practical effect is income splitting. Under this approach married couples would add up all their income and then split it into halves. Each spouse would then file as a single individual and pay tax on half of the total income using the standard deduction and tax rate brackets for single individuals.

Assuming the current tax rate schedules, either one of these approaches would give all married taxpayers a tax cut equal to the largest possible marriage tax penalty that could occur at any given income level. Married couples would all receive a tax cut regardless of whether or not they currently incur a marriage tax penalty. This means that married couples who currently receive a marriage tax bonus (they pay less filing a joint return than they would filing two single returns) would have their bonus increased. Other married couples would move from the penalty category into the bonus category.

These approaches would create a singles' tax penalty (one's income tax liability would always go down by getting married) and therefore, in some regards, would move the income tax system further away from marriage neutrality than it is under the current system. Since, it is estimated that in 1998, there were 72 million tax returns filed by single individuals and heads of households versus 49 million returns filed by married couples, adopting an approach that would be perceived by many as creating a large singles' tax penalty might produce a negative reaction. These approaches would probably entail the largest revenue costs of the major options under consideration.

Increasing the Standard Deduction for Joint Returns

While increasing the standard deduction for joint returns so that it is twice the amount of the standard deduction for single returns would be a far less costly option than full income splitting, it would not make the tax system marriage neutral. Although this approach would eliminate the marriage tax penalty for some married couples who do not itemize and mitigate the penalty for other couples who do not itemize, it would increase the marriage tax bonuses for other married couples and not affect couples who do not use the standard deduction, i.e itemize, and who currently pay a tax penalty.

However, since almost 60% of joint returns see all of their income taxed at the 15% tax bracket, simply increasing the joint standard deduction to twice the amount of the single standard deduction would mean that marriage tax penalties (excluding those introduced by the EITC) would be eliminated for the majority of joint returns.

DEVELOPMENTS IN THE 107TH CONGRESS

As part of his overall tax cut plan, President Bush has proposed a two-earner marital deduction of 10% of the lower earning spouse's income with a maximum deduction of $3,000. The two-earner marital deduction would be phased in over a five year period.

In late March 2001, the House passed H.R. 6 which contained marriage tax penalty relief. Under H.R. 6 the standard deduction for joint returns would be increased to twice the amount of the standard deduction for single returns, effective beginning 2002. It would increase the width of the 15% tax bracket for joint returns to twice the width of the 15% tax bracket for single returns. This change would be phased in over the period 2004 to 2009. Finally, H.R. 6 would allow married taxpayers who file a joint return to increase the earned income amount used to calculate the earned income tax credit (EITC) to 110% of their earned income

APPENDIX A: CONFLICTING EQUITY GOALS

To demonstrate the logical inconsistences of these three concepts of equity (marriage neutrality, progressivity, and equal taxation of couples with equal incomes) consider the case of these four taxpayers Andy (A), Betty (B), Cathy (C), and David (D) expressed in an algebraic form. A and B each have incomes of $30,000, C has no income, and D has an income of $60,000. If the tax system is progressive (as opposed to proportional), then the combined tax on A and B cannot equal the tax on D (if the taxes were equal then the tax system would be proportional). Hence:

(1) $T(A) + T(B) \cdot T(D)$

At the same time, for the tax system to be marriage neutral, then the tax on A and B, if they got married, should be the same as their combined tax liabilities as two singles. Hence:

(2) $T(A) + T(B) = T(A+B)$

In addition, to qualify as marriage neutral, the tax on C and D, if they got married should be the same as the tax on D as a single individual (since C had no income and no tax). Hence:

(3) $T(C) + T(D) = T(C+D)$

To achieve the goal that couples with equal incomes pay equal tax requires that the tax on A and B should equal the tax on C and D. Hence:

(4) $T(A+B) = T(C+D)$

Substituting equations (2) and (3) into equation (4) produces:

(5) $T(A) + T(B) = T(D)$

Equation (5) however, contradicts equation (1), which says that for the tax system to be progressive, the combined tax on A and B cannot equal the tax on D. This algebraic representation demonstrates the fact that the tax system can be marriage neutral and tax couples with equal incomes equally only under a proportional tax, but not under a progressive tax.

APPENDIX B: TAX RATE SCHEDULES FOR 2000

Statutory Marginal Tax Rates, Personal Exemptions, And Standard Deductions, 2000

Personal Exemptions	$2,800
Standard Deductions	
Joint	$7,350
Single	4,400
Head of Household	6,450

Additional Standard Deductions for the Elderly and the Blind	
Joint	$850
Single/Head of Household	1,100

Marginal Income Tax Rates

If *taxable income* is:	Then, *tax* is:
Joint Returns	
$ 0 - $ 43,850	15% of the amount over $ 0
$ 43,850 - $ 105,950	$6,578 + 28% of the amount over $43,850
$ 105,950 - $ 161,450	$23,966 + 31% of the amount over $105,950
$ 161,450 - $ 288,350	$41,171 + 36% of the amount over $161,450
$ 288,350 +	$86,855 + 39.6% of the amount over $288,350

If *taxable income* is:	Then, *tax* is:
Single Returns	
$ 0 - $ 26,250	15% of the amount over $ 0
$ 26,250 - $ 63,550	$3,938 + 28% of the amount over $26,250
$ 63,550 - $ 132,600	$14,382 + 31% of the amount over $63,550
$ 132,600 - $ 288,350	$35,787 + 36% of the amount over $132,600
$ 288,350 +	$91,857 + 39.6% of the amount over $288,350

If *taxable income* is:	Then, *tax* is:
Heads of Households	
$ 0 - $ 35,150	15% of the amount over $ 0
$ 35,150 - $ 90,800	$5,273 + 28% of the amount over $35,150
$ 90,800 - $ 147,050	$20,855 + 31% of the amount over $90,800
$ 147,050 - $ 288,350	$38,292 + 36% of the amount over $147,050
$ 288,350 +	$89,160 + 39.6% of the amount over $288,350

Chapter 9

DEFENSE OF MARRIAGE ACT: DISSENTING VIEWS*

John Conyers, Jr., Barney Frank, Howard L. Berman, Jerrold Nadler, Melvin L. Watt, Zoe Lofgren, Maxine Waters, Patricia Schroeder and Xavier Becerra

Supporters of the legislation which they have named the 'Defense of Marriage Act' assert that it is necessary essentially as a states rights measure. That is, they claim that if we do not pass this bill into law this year, states all over the country will be compelled by a decision of the courts in Hawaii to legalize same sex marriage. Very little of this is in fact true, and one of the major problems with this bill is that, contrary to its supporters assertions that it is intended to defend the rights of states, the bill will severely undercut state authority in the area of marriage, in part explicitly and in part implicitly.

DESCRIPTION OF LEGISLATION AND SUMMARY

H.R. 3936 has two distinct parts. Sec. 2 amends 28 U.S.C. 1738 by adding a new section, 1738C, to provide that '[n]o State, territory or possession shall be required to give effect to any public act, record, or judicial proceeding of any other State, territory, possession, or tribe respecting a relationship between persons of the same sex that is treated as a marriage under the laws of such other State, territory, possession, or tribe, or a right or claim arising from such relationship.'

Sec. 3 defines marriage for Federal purposes, by providing that 'marriage' means only a legal union between one man and one woman as husband and wife, and the word 'spouse' refers only to a person of the opposite sex who is a husband or a wife.'

The first thing that should be noted is that there is no emergency here. The legislation is offered as a 'response' to a Hawaii Supreme Court case, *Baehr* v. *Lewin*,[1] issued more than three years ago, which remanded a same sex marriage claim back to a Hawaii trial court for a determination of whether denial of a marriage license was a violation of the Hawaii Constitution's equal protection guarantee based on gender. The trial court is not scheduled to begin hearing the case until September of this year, with appeals continuing for well beyond next year. Thus, while H.R. 3396 is characterized as a response to an 'imminent' threat of same sex marriage being forced on the nation by several judges of the Hawaii Supreme Court (and to the rest of the nation through the claimed legal compulsion of the of the Full Faith and Credit clause), in fact there is nothing imminent. There is no likelihood that Hawaii will complete this process until well into next year at the earliest, giving us plenty of time to legislate with more thought and analysis.

In no jurisdiction in this nation is same sex marriage recognized by law. To the contrary, as of today, 14 states have enacted laws which in some fashion make explicit those states' objection to same sex marriages. This federal legislation is therefore an unwarranted response to a non-issue.

Second, the argument that if Hawaii does finally decide to recognize same sex marriages, this legislation is necessary--or even useful--in helping other states reject that as their own policy is not only wrong, it is a proposition which the sponsors of this legislation do not themselves genuinely believe.

The legal history of the full faith and credit clause which is central to this dispute is a sparse one, and no one can speak with absolute certainly about all aspects of this matter. But one thing is quite clear: whatever powers states have to reject a decision by another state to legalize same sex

---

* Excerpted from House Report 104-664 at www.house.gov.
[1] 852 P.2d 44 (Haw. 1993)]

marriage, and to refuse to recognize such marriages within its own borders, derives directly from the Constitution and nothing Congress can do by statute either adds to or detracts from that power. That is, the prevailing view today is that states can by adopting their own contrary policies deny recognition to marriages of a type of which they disapprove, and it is incontestable that states have in fact done this on policy grounds in the past. Support for this fact is so clear that constitutional scholars not often in agreement on this point agree. See, e.g., Professor Laurence Tribe's letter to Senator Kennedy, May 23, 1996, and Bruce Fein's 'Defending a Sacred Covenant,' The legal Times, June 17, 1996. And most relevant for the purposes of this discussion is that states have in the past been free to reject the demand that they recognize marriages from other states because of policy reasons without any intervention whatsoever by the federal government.

Indeed, given that the power that states have to reject marriages of which they disapprove on policy grounds derives directly from the Constitution and has never previously been held to need any Congressional authorization, the fact that Congress in this proposed statute presumes to give the states permission to do what virtually all states think they already now have the power to do undercuts states rights. If entities--individuals, states, or any other--have a Constitutional right to take certain actions, then the effect of Congress passing a statute which gives them permission to do what they already have the right to do serves not to empower them, but to undercut in the minds of some the power they already have. This point has been argued with particular force by Professor Laurence Tribe in the letter he sent to Senator Kennedy, a copy of which has been inserted into the record of the proceedings on this bill in the Judiciary Committee. A more detailed legal analysis of this matter is as follows.

TREATMENT OF OUT OF STATE MARRIAGES GOVERNED GENERALLY BY CHOICE OF LAW RULES

Notwithstanding the language of the Full Faith and Credit clause, Article IV, Section 1:

Full Faith and Credit shall be given in each State to the public Act, Records, and judicial Proceedings of every other State. And the Congress may be general Laws prescribe the Manner in which such Acts, Records, and Proceedings shall be proved, and the Effect thereof.

The clause has had its principal operation in relation only to judgments.

It is settled constitutional law that the final judgment of one state must be recognized in another state, and that a second state's interest in the adjudicated matter is limited to questions of authenticity, and personal jurisdiction, i.e., notwithstanding the first court's assertion of jurisdiction, proof that the first court lacked jurisdiction may be collaterally impeached in a second state's court.[2]

Again, notwithstanding the plain language of the clause, recognition of rights based upon State Constitutions, statutes and common laws are treated differently than judgments. 'With regard to the extrastate protection of rights which have not matured into final judgments, the full faith and credit clause has never abolished the general principal of the dominance of local policy over the rules of comity.'[3]

Alaska Packers Assn v. *Comm,*[4] elaborated on this doctrine, holding that where statute or policy of the forum State is set up as a defense to a suit brought under the statute of another State or territory, or where a foreign statute is set up as a defense to a suit or proceedings under a local statute, the conflict is to be resolved, not by giving automatic effect to the full faith and credit clause and thus compelling courts of each State to subordinate its own statutes to those of others but by appraising the governmental interest of each jurisdiction and deciding accordingly.

Marriage licensure is not a judgment.[5] Therefore, the Full Faith and Credit clause does not, under traditional analysis, have anything to say about sister state recognition of marriage.

The Supreme Court has not yet passed on the manner in which marriages per se are entitled to full faith and credit, even though it would appear from the face of the clause they should be afforded full faith and credit as either Acts or Records.

In the absence of an express constitutional protection under full faith and credit, state courts (and Federal courts) rely on traditional choice of law/conflict of law rules. The general rule for determining the validity of a

---

[2] *Williams* v. *North Carolina* II, 325 U.S. 226 (1945). See also, *Esenwein* v. *Commonwealth,* 325 U.S. 279 (1945).

[3] Congressional Research Serv., Library of Congress, The Constitution of the United States of America, Analysis and Interpretation, at 859 (1987), citing, *Bond* v. *Hume,* 243 U.S. 15 (1917).

[4] 294 U.S. 532 (1935).

[5] That is not to say that marriage could not in some cases be converted to a judgment, as when a marriage is in dispute and the parties go to court and seek a decree validating the marriage.

marriage legally created and recognized in another jurisdiction is to apply the law of the state in which the marriage was performed. [6]

There are two strong exceptions to this choice of law rule: first, a court will not recognize a marriage performed in another state if a statute of the forum state clearly expresses that the general rule of validation should not be applied to such marriages, and, second, a court will refuse to recognize a valid foreign marriage if the recognition of that marriage would violate a strongly held public policy of the forum state. [7]

Those states which desire to avoid the general rule favoring application of the law where the marriage was celebrated will rely on an enumerated public policy exception to the rule: through state statute, common law, or practice the state will show that honoring a sister state's celebration of marriage 'would be the approval of a transaction which is inherently vicious, wicked, or immoral, and shocking to the prevailing moral sense.'[8] The rhetoric notwithstanding, the public policy exception has not been a difficult hurdle to overcome for states, subject to the limitations of other constitutional provisions, to wit, equal protection, substantive due process, etc. States could show their public policy exception to same sex marriage by offering gender specific marriage laws, anti-sodomy statutes, common law, etc.

Different courts have required different levels of clarity in their own states expression of public policy before that exception could be sustained in that states' court. Some have required explicit statutory expression,[9] while others much less clearly so. [10]

Courts have considered a marriage offensive to a state's public policy either because it is contrary to natural law or because it violates a positive law enacted by the state legislature. Courts have invalidated incestuous, polygamous, and interracial foreign marriages on the ground that they violate natural law.[11] For invalidation based on positive law, some courts have required clear statutory expressions that the marriages prohibited are void regardless of where they are performed,[12] and sometimes a clear intent to preempt the general rule of validation.[13] Other courts have set up not so

---

[6] Ehrenzweig, A Treatise on the Conflict of Laws, sec. 138 (1961).

[7] Restatement (Second) Conflict of Laws sec. 283 (1971).

[8] *Intercontinental Hotels Corp.* v. *Golden*, 203 N.E.2d 210, 212 (N.Y. 1964).]

[9] *Etheridge* v. *Shaddock*, 706 S.W.2d 396 (Ark. 1986).

[10] *Condado Aruba Caribbean Hotel* v. *Tickel*, 561 P.2d 23, 24 (Colo. Ct. App. 1977).

[11] See, e.g., *Earle* v. *Earle*, 126 N.Y.S. 317, 319 (1910).

[12] *State* v. *Graves* 307 S.W.2d 545 (Ark. 1957).

[13] See, e.g., Estate of Loughmiller, 629 P.2d 156 (Kas. 1981).

high a hurdle, such that a statutory enactment against the substantive issue was sufficient.[14] Those states that are enacting anti-same sex marriage statutes may well find they have satisfied the first exception to the choice of law rule validating a marriage where celebrated.

Interracial marriages were, before *Loving* v. *Virginia,* treated with the above choice of law analysis, and 'courts frequently determined the validity of interracial marriages based on an analysis of the public policy exception. Early decisions treated such marriages as contrary to natural law, but later courts considered the question one of positive law interpretation.'[15]

Other examples of common public policy exception analyses include common law marriages, persons under the age permitted by a forum's marriage statute, and statutes which prohibit persons from remarrying within a certain period.

The Uniform Marriage and Divorce Act, effective in at least seventeen states, provides that '[a]ll marriages contracted within this State prior to the effective date of the act, or outside this State, that were valid at the time of the contract or subsequently validated by the laws of the place in which they were contracted or by the domicile of the parties, are valid in this State.'[16] The Act specifically drops the public policy exception: 'the section expressly fails to incorporate the 'strong public policy' exception to the Restatement and thus may change the law in some jurisdictions. This section will preclude invalidation of many marriages which would have been invalidated of many marriages which would have been invalidated in the past.'[17] Of course, any state that wants to reassert a public policy exception for same sex marriages retains the right to so legislate, or not. The proposed federal bill has no effect on that.

CONSTITUTIONAL RESTRAINTS

There are several possible Constitutional limits on a states' ability to invoke a public policy exception to the general rule of validating foreign

---

[14] *Catalano* v. *Catalano,* 170 A.2d 726 (Conn. 1961)(finding express prohibitions in a marriage statute and the criminalization of incestuous marriages sufficient to invalidate an out of state marriage).]
[15] Hovermill, 53 Md. L. Rev. 450 (1994), at 464.
[16] 9A U.L.A. sec. 210 (1979).
[17] Id., official comment.

marriages: the due process clause, equal protection, the effects clause of the Full Faith and Credit clause, or substantive due process.

For due process, the second state must before it can apply its own law satisfy that it has 'significant contact or a significant aggregation of contracts' with the parties and the occurrence or transaction to which it is applying its own law.[18] The contacts necessary to survive a due process challenge have been characterized as 'incidental.'[19]

Substantive due process and equal protection can bar a state's application of a public policy exception as well. For the former, a court would have to find that there is a fundamental right for homosexuals to marry. There is complete agreement that there is a fundamental right to marry,[20] and the argument will be pursued that this incorporates marriage of homosexuals to each other. There has been never been such a holding in any federal or state court, including even the Hawaii case, *Baehr* v. *Lewin*. [21]

For equal protection analysis a state's anti same sex marriage statute could be subjected to one of three levels of scrutiny.[22] If it is viewed as almost all statutory enactments, under rational basis, the state will in all likelihood have to show more than animus motivates the restrictive legislation. If an argument can be persuasive that the anti same sex marriage statute is discrimination based on gender, it may well receive intermediate scrutiny. No court has been persuaded that anti same sex marriage laws are gender based discrimination.[23] For strict scrutiny, the court would have to for the first time elevate classifications based on homosexuality to that of strict scrutiny, a level which may be due, but nowhere operative.

If the Full Faith and Credit clause requires recognition, as it does for judgments, there is no Constitutional exception to that requirement, and most certainly Congress could not create one by statute.

Professor Tribe makes this point and then argues that the attempt to do so legislatively is itself unconstitutional. And Congress' disability is the same for substantive due process: if there were found to exist a substantive due process bar to a state's prohibition of same-sex marriage, no Congressional enactment could affect that, it would be a matter between the States and the Supreme Court interpreting the United States Constitution.

---

[18] *Allstate Ins. Co.* v. *Hague*, 449 U.S. 302 (1981).
[19] 53 Md. L. Rev. at 467.
[20] *Zablocki* v. *Redhail*, 434 U.S. 374 (1978).
[21] 852 P.2d 44, 57 (Haw. 1993).
[22] *City of Cleburne* v. *Cleburne Living Center*, 473 U.S. 432 (1985).
[23] See, e.g., *Baker* v. *Nelson*, 191 N.W.2d 185 (Minn. 1971).

The policy/doctrinal analog to Professor Tribe's constitutional argument is the following: while the proponents purport to be protecting States' rights and interests, they are in fact diluting those rights and interests. The clear expression in this legislation that the Congress has a role in determining when a state may not offer full faith and credit creates a standard of Federal control antithetical to conservative philosophy and the Tenth Amendment: that powers not enumerated for the Federal Government are reserved to the States. This legislation enumerates a Federal power, namely the power to deny sister state recognition, grants that power to the state, and therefore dangerously pronounces, expressio unius est exclusio alterius, that the Federal government in fact retains the power to limit full faith and credit. And it only need express that power substantive issue by substantive issue. This is an arrogation of power to the federal government which one would have assumed heretical to the expressed philosophy of conservative legislating. Under the guise of protecting states' interests, the proposed statutes would infringe upon state sovereignty and effectively transfer broad power to the federal government.

As to the second prong of Full Faith and Credit, only rarely has Congress exercised the implementing authority which the Clause grants to it. The first, passed in 1790,[24] provides for ways to authenticate acts, records and judicial proceedings, and repeats the constitutional injunction that such acts, records and judicial proceedings of the states are entitled to full faith and credit in other states, as well as by the federal government. The second, dating from 1804, provides methods of authenticating non-judicial records.[25]

Since 1804 these provisions have been amended only twice, the Parental Kidnapping Prevention Act of 1980,[26] which provides that custody determinations of a state shall be enforced in different states, and 28 U.S.C.A. Sec. 1738B, 'Full Faith and Credit for Child Support Orders' (1994). Neither of these statutes purported to limit full faith and credit; to the contrary, each of these statutes reinforced or expanded the faith and credit given to states' court orders.

Full Faith and Credit, discussed above, provides little break on the application of a sister states' policies, as opposed to judgments.[27] Again, full

[24] 28 U.S.C.A. sec. 1738.
[25] 28 U.S.C.A. sec. 1739.
[26] 28 U.S.C.A. sec. 1739A.
[27] *Carroll* v. *Lanza,* 349 U.S. 408 (1955)('Arkansas can adopt Missouri's policy if she likes. Or * * * she may supplement it or displace it with another, insofar as remedies for acts occurring within her boundaries are concerned').

faith and credit with respect to states' policies (not judgments) has merged with due process analysis, and as long as a state has significant contacts it may apply its own law.

The privileges and immunities clause[28] is irrelevant here because of the various interpretations one could imbue to the face of the language, the Supreme Court has settled on that which merely forbids any State to discriminate against citizens of other States in favor of its own. It is this narrow interpretation which has become the settled one. [29]

Section three of the bill, ironically for legislation which has been hailed as a defender of states rights, represents for the first time in our history a Congressional effort, if successful, to deny states full discretion over their own marriage laws. Section three of this bill says that no matter what an individual state says, and no matter by what procedure it does it, Congress will refuse to recognize same sex marriages. In debating against an amendment by Congresswoman Schroeder, described below, one of the Senior Republicans on the Committee said that her amendment would make certain marriages 'second class marriages' by denying them federal recognition. This acknowledgment that denying a marriage federal recognition substantially diminishes its legal force applies to this bill. If Hawaii or any other state were to allow people of the same sex who were deeply and emotionally attached to each other to regularize that relationship in a marriage, this bill says that the federal government would refuse to recognize it. Note that this is the case whether such decision is made by a State Supreme Court, a referendum of the state's population, a vote of the state's legislature, or some combination thereof. Thus, the bill is exactly the opposite of a states rights measure: the only real force it will have will be to deny a state and the people of that state the right to make decisions on the question of same sex marriage.

Our final ground for opposing this bill is our vehement disagreement with the notion that same sex marriages are a threat to marriage. By far the weakest part of this bill logically is its title, but its title is not simply accidental, but rather reflects the calculated political judgment that went into introducing this bill at this time, months before a national election, and rushing it through with inadequate analysis of its impact. That this bill's consequences are not adequately analyzed was conceded by members of the majority who spoke in its defense, when they argued that we must deny

---

[28] The Citizens of each State shall be entitled to all Privileges and Immunities of Citizens in the several States.

recognition to same sex marriages declared by states to be legal because we do not know what the implications of this will be for various federal programs. In a rational legislative atmosphere not shaped largely by electoral considerations, committees of the Congress would be holding hearings on the various aspects of this so that we would not have to use ignorance as an excuse for haste.

The notion that allowing two people who are in love to become legally responsible to and for each other threatens heterosexual marriage is without factual basis. Indeed, when pressed during Subcommittee and Committee debate, majority Members could give no specific content to this assertion. The attraction that a man and a woman feel for each other, which leads them to wish to commit emotionally and legally to each other for life, obviously could not be threatened in any way, shape or form by the love that two other people feel for each other, whether they be people of the same sex or opposite sexes. There are of course problems which men and women who seek to marry, or seek to maintain a marriage, confront in our society. No one anywhere has produced any evidence, or even argued logically, that the existence of same sex couples is one of those difficulties. And to prove that this is simply an effort to capitalize on the public dislike of the notion of same sex marriages, as noted below, when Congresswoman Schroeder attempted to offer amendments that deal more directly with threats to existing heterosexual marriages, the majority unanimously and vehemently objected.

JUDICIARY COMMITTEE CONSIDERATION

During Judiciary Committee consideration of the legislation, four amendments were offered, none of which was approved. One amendment, offered by Mr. Frank of Massachusetts, would have struck from the bill Section 3, which defines for Federal purposes marriage as a legal union between a man and woman.

Supporters of this amendment recognized that the Federal government has always relied on the states' definition of marriage for Federal purposes, and that it is unwarranted and an intrusion on states rights to change that practice now. The Federal government has no history in determining the legal status of relationships, and to begin to do so now is a derogation of

---

[29] *Whitfield* v. *Ohio*, 297 U.S. 431 (1936).

states' traditional right to so determine. One objection to this amendment centered around the argument that several justices of the Hawaii Supreme Court could possibly determine policy for the nation (which assumes an interpretation of the Full Faith and Credit Clause with respect to marriages which has no current foundation), so the Federal government must put the brakes on 'judicial activism.'

Mr. Frank met this objection with a subsequent amendment, which provided that were a state to determine by citizen initiative, referendum or legislation that the definition of marriage for that state would be different than that which is enumerated in H.R. 3396, that states' definition would apply for its own residents for Federal purposes. This amendment obviated the non-argument about 'judicial activism,' and placed a clear question of states rights before the Judiciary Committee. That is, were a state to decide through its normal legislative process that same sex marriage was valid in that state, Federal application would follow accordingly for citizens of that state.

In addition to the fact that nowhere is same sex marriage ready to be enacted into law, if the citizens of Hawaii determine that they disagree with their Supreme Court, the mechanism to undo that possible Supreme Court ruling is clear: Hawaii law provides that a constitutional amendment may go to the voters if both Chambers of the Hawaii legislature pass it by 2/3 majority, or, if in two successive sessions both Chambers pass it by simple majority. In fact, the legislature of Hawaii has responded to the pending litigation there. In 1996 the Hawaii House of Representatives passed, 37-14, an amendment to Hawaii's constitution which would have defined marriage as a lawful union between a man and a woman. The Hawaii Senate then defeated the House passed amendment, 15-10.

The second Frank amendment was defeated in Committee, and the supporters of H.R. 3396 were confronted with the unadorned core of their motives: they are not at all interested in giving citizens the effect of their democratic choices or even in respecting what are historically states rights, rather, supporters of the legislation are using the Congressional process as a platform to express their moral objection to people of the same sex committing to each other, loving each other, expressing love and mutual responsibility for each other, and agreeing to provide for each other.

Mrs. Schroeder offered two amendments which were intended to address real threats to marriage. One amendment would have modified the Federal definition of marriage within the legislation to include 'monogamous', such that a marriage, otherwise a legal union in a state, would not be eligible for that status for Federal purposes if the relationship between the man and the woman was not monogamous. Ms. Jackson Lee offered a friendly amendment to the amendment, which modified 'monogamous' with the words 'non-adulterous'. Mrs. Schroeder argued that same sex relationship were no threat to heterosexual marriages, but non-monogamous and adulterous relationships were.

Mrs. Schroeder offered a second amendment which would have also narrowed the Federal definition of marriage of exclude those legal unions between man and women in which either of the parties has previously been granted a divorce which was not determined on fault grounds and in which property and support issues were not resolved in accordance with fault findings. Mrs. Schroeder argued, again, that same sex marriage was no threat to any heterosexual marriage, but that if supporters of the legislation in fact wanted to 'defend' marriage, that the ease with which people could exit marriage should be examined.

Her argument was that too lax rules ('no-fault', in some circumstances) permitted a system in which significant numbers of people were abandoned by former spouses who then were left without financial contributions from the departing spouse, coupled with too lax intervention by state and federal governments for the collection of alimony and child support left many people without adequate support, and relying on the Government for their welfare. If one was truly interested in defending the institution of marriage, Mrs. Schroeder argued, then support for tightening the procedure for exiting that institution, or in this case, narrowing the Federal status of marriage for any person who benefited from the lax exit rules, was in order. Her amendment was defeated, but in the process supporters of the legislation admitted that their purported motivation to 'defend' marriage was somewhat narrower than the title of the legislation implies.

CONCLUSION

The 'Defense of Marriage Act' is insupportable. It is legally unnecessary and as a policy matter unwise. The effect of the legislation will be not to protect heterosexual marriage, an institution we strongly support, but rather to divide people needlessly and to diminish the power of states to determine their own laws with respect to marriage. For these reasons, we oppose the measure.

Chapter 10

AMERICA IS AT A MORAL CROSSROADS*

Terry Everett

The headlines say it all: "Gay Marriage is a Right...," "FCC Ok's F-Word", "Judges Ban Pledge of Allegiance from Schools..." These are taken from recent news stories and reflect what many believe is evidence that America is now at a moral crossroads.

Last week, the national media broke the news that the Massachusetts Supreme Court has ruled in favor of same-sex marriages in that state. While the issue is by no means settled, it sets the stage for the battle over redefinition of marriage in America. The institution of marriage is the foundation of the family. And families play a critical role in raising our children, the future of our society.

According to recent polls, a majority of Americans believe that marriage should be reserved as a legal union between men and women. I agree, and accordingly have cosponsored H.J. Res. 56, the Federal Marriage Amendment. It would amend the Constitution to state that "marriage in the United States shall consist only of the union of a man and a woman." I am also on record as supporting the Defense of Marriage Act that passed into law in 1996. It protects marriage as a male-female bond and allows states to refuse to recognize same-sex marriages which might be legal in other states.

Same-sex marriage partners are also ineligible for survivors benefits under Federal veterans and Social Security programs, or to file joint tax returns.

Last month, many were shocked to read that the Federal Communications Commission (FCC) has allowed the broadcast of offensive language that was formerly prohibited. Specifically, the FCC ruled October 3 that the "F-word" could be spoken on broadcast radio and television provided it is not used to depict "sexual or excretory activities." The Commission made the ruling in response to hundreds of protests from the use of this profane word by U2's Bono during the January Golden Globe Awards aired on national television.

I have received hundreds of emails from citizens of Southeast Alabama who are understandably outraged by the FCC's action. Clearly, it sets the precedent for the use of foul language on any radio and television channel at any hour of the day and night. This is unacceptable and I have conveyed my displeasure to the FCC. I understand the Commission is currently reviewing its decision.

Last year, the Ninth U.S. Circuit Court of Appeals in San Francisco ruled the Pledge of Allegiance unconstitutional and could not be recited in classrooms because of its inclusion of the words "under God." I have cosponsored legislation in the U.S. House to make the Pledge off limits to court action, effectively protecting it. The Pledge Protection Act was introduced on May 8 and has 222 cosponsors.

Isn't it ironic that a Federal court can prohibit the utterance of "under God" in our schools, yet the "F-word" is now acceptable in many broadcasts? Isn't it ironic that the sacred, time-honored institution of marriage is being undermined by the courts' twisted interpretation of "rights", yet the Ten Commandments are banned from public display? Liberals clamor against prayer in schools while jealously guarding the right of record companies and Hollywood moviemakers to churn out music, videos and games glorifying sex and violence.

It's time Americans woke up to the forces that are slowly seeking to transform our country. That means putting the courts, the media, and Hollywood on notice. Only then will your voice be heard and our moral traditions protected for future generations.

Chapter 11

CONSTITUTION PROVIDES KEY TO PROTECTING MARRIAGE[*]

John Hostettler

Bowing to the demands of four unelected members of its state supreme court, Massachusetts recently began issuing marriage licenses to men who want to marry men, women who want to wed women.

As other states and municipalities follow Massachusetts' lead, this cultural battle will inevitably end up in federal court. And unless action is taken, it's probably just a matter of time before a federal judge rules that homosexual "marriages" should be recognized nationwide.

As we've seen in decisions ranging from abortion to the public expression of religion, judges clearly no longer feel an obligation to connect their opinions to the U.S. Constitution or the laws of the land. In fact, the courts have started citing the laws and judicial proceedings of foreign governments to defend their findings.

And they insist their rulings are final.

That would come as news to our nation's founders, who envisioned a government of the people, not a government of black-robed rulers. The Constitution they designed established a government of divided authority with clear, unambiguous roles reserved for each of the three branches.

---

[*] Excerpted from http://www.house.gov/hostettler/Issues/Hostettler-issues-2004-05-19-Constitution-Protects-Marriage.htm.

But today we're told that when the court violates the Constitution there is no recourse short of amending the Constitution. Congress, the executive branch and the people must simply live with its decision.

This is a myth. Judges can't force their will upon the people because the Constitution doesn't provide them with a single tool to make their rulings become reality. Unconstitutional judicial decisions only have effect if Congress and the president allow them to.

Alexander Hamilton, in a 1788 essay promoting adoption of the U.S. Constitution, says it well: "[T]he judiciary is beyond comparison the weakest of the three departments of power. The judiciary has no influence over either the sword or the purse. . . and can take no active resolution whatever. It may truly be said to have neither force nor will but merely judgment; ..." [emphasis added.]

The Founders, in their wisdom, recognized that power corrupts. So they established Constitutional mechanisms to prevent one branch from assuming too much authority. They allowed the court, within parameters, to make judgements, but left lawmaking, funding and enforcement to the stronger, elected branches.

The Constitution grants three specific powers to the Legislature and Executive that were not granted to the Courts.

The first is the power to enforce the law, which is granted exclusively to the president in Article II, Section 3.

In other words, without the aid of the executive branch, a court ruling granting a right to homosexual marriage is moot, especially since the Constitution prohibits the president from executing a court order inconsistent with the Constitution.

The Judiciary, as Hamilton said, is left with "merely judgment" that "must ultimately depend upon the aid of the executive arm even for the efficacy of its judgments."

The second constitutional power denied the courts is the legislative spending power granted exclusively to Congress in Article 1, section 9. Simply put, if Congress does not fund a thing, that thing does not happen.

So if a federal court opines that the Constitution grants homosexuals the right to have their Massachusetts' marriage license recognized in Indiana, Congress can simply deny the funds to enforce that decision. The House did this very thing last year when it overwhelmingly passed amendments I offered denying funds to enforce court decisions banning the Pledge of Allegiance and the public depiction of the Ten Commandments.

The third power granted to Congress and denied to the courts is the authority to limit the jurisdiction of federal courts on specific topics. The Framers of the Constitution made explicit provision for this type of check in the Constitution itself. Article I, Section 8 and Article III, Sections 1 and 2 grant Congress the authority to establish inferior federal courts, determine their jurisdiction and make exceptions to the Supreme Court's appellate jurisdiction.

I believe this authority is the most effective way to prevent the federal courts from creating a federal "right" for homosexuals to marry each other. So I introduced the Marriage Protection Act (H.R. 3313), which removes jurisdiction from certain federal courts over questions pertaining to the 1996 Defense of Marriage Act, better known as DOMA.

DOMA says that no state is required to give full faith and credit to a marriage license issued by another state if that relationship is between two people of the same sex. It also defines the terms "marriage" and "spouse" for purposes of federal law as terms only applying to relationships between people of the opposite sex.

DOMA is good law and passed with broad support, but an imaginative federal court could easily opine that a fundamental "right" to homosexual marriage exists somewhere in the U.S. Constitution and order Hoosiers to recognize a marriage license granted to homosexuals "married" in Massachusetts.

The Marriage Protection Act addresses that possibility by removing the Supreme Court's appellate jurisdiction, as well as inferior federal courts' original and appellate jurisdiction, over DOMA's full faith and credit provision.

Simply put, if federal courts don't have jurisdiction over marriage issues, they can't hear them. And if they can't hear cases regarding marriage policy, they can't redefine this sacred institution and establish a national precedent for homosexual marriage.

Thirty-eight states already protect traditional marriage under DOMA. By exercising this Constitutional legislative authority we can preserve each state's traditional right to determine its own marriage policies without federal court interference.

There is a radical element in America working to change our dictionaries, our Bibles, our traditions and our laws. But it's not the institution of marriage that needs redefining. It is our understanding of the federal courts and the limitations placed on them by the U.S. Constitution.

Equipped with knowledge, the American people can reclaim the governance that is rightfully theirs.

INDEX